Gustav Karpeles

A Sketch of Jewish History

Gustav Karpeles

A Sketch of Jewish History

ISBN/EAN: 9783337029531

Printed in Europe, USA, Canada, Australia, Japan

Cover: Foto ©ninafisch / pixelio.de

More available books at **www.hansebooks.com**

Special Series No. 5

A
SKETCH OF JEWISH HISTORY

BY

GUSTAV KARPELES

TRANSLATED FROM THE GERMAN

PHILADELPHIA
THE JEWISH PUBLICATION SOCIETY OF AMERICA
1897

PREFATORY NOTE

The following lectures, translated from the German, were delivered by Doctor Karpeles during the winter of 1895-96 before the lodges of the Independent Order *B'ne B'rith* at Berlin. The translation is done from stenographic notes printed as manuscript and not published. A few slight changes have been made.

A brief and graphic sketch like this necessarily brings the individual views of the writer into great prominence. There may be room for other views diverging widely from his. The Committee believes, however, that the work will be useful in stimulating readers of Jewish History to a renewed and more vigilant examination of the subject in works they have not read carefully, as well as in the great work of Graetz, with which all have a certain familiarity.

I

A SOLITARY little vessel is drifting on a vast ocean; neither wind nor wave can do it harm. Ofttimes the mountain-high billows seem about to suck it into their swirl and sink it to the bottom of the sea; but ever again it rides upon the crests of the waves, serenely sailing on in its course. Under this metaphor our sages of old conceived the history of Israel. Israel is the tiny craft sailing in loneliness across a boundless ocean. Again and again he seems about to be engulfed by the nations; again and again it looks as though Israel were stricken forever from the list of the peoples of earth, but he always reappears, rejuvenated, with added numbers, with increased strength.

To draw a picture, however sketchlike, of Israel's history from its earliest beginnings to the present time, it is necessary to divide it up into several periods. Naturally, the boundary lines between the periods cannot be sharply drawn. As it is, text-books of history have too long held to the traditional division into the epochs known as ancient times, middle ages, and the modern period. In point of fact, the ancient times overlap the so-called middle ages, which in turn trench upon the modern period. The division hitherto accepted must sooner or later be abandoned. Historians treating of Israel's vicissitudes are more favorably situated.

<small>Epochs of Jewish History</small>

Israel's antiquity is a well-defined period; it comes to a close on a certain day, that on which the destruction of Jerusalem and the loss of national independence occurred. The mediæval period was of great length, reaching down even into the last century. The reader can, therefore, judge for himself of how long a modern period we have the right to speak.

Closer inspection of the history of Israel, however, reveals six great periods, the end of each marked either by the removal of his activity to a new scene, or by a change of his attitude towards the problems of the spiritual life.

The *first* of these periods naturally is that extending from the earliest glimmering of historical consciousness to the destruction of the First Temple and the Captivity of Israel in Babylonia, the period to be considered in this paper. The return of the Babylonian exiles to Jerusalem and their fortunes until the total annihilation of national independence are embraced in the history of the *second* period, the most remarkable and the most important in the life of Israel, who, in its course, originated a new religion, Christianity.

The *third* period covers nearly ten centuries, during which the amazing intellectual work deposited in the two Talmuds and their cognate literature was accomplished. The *fourth* period opens with the real diaspora, the great migration of Israel from the Orient, in quest of a new home among the nations, which he found with the Arabs of Spain and northern Africa, where the Jewish mind unfolded in new and prolific beauty, and gave to the mediæval periods of Israel's history their characteristic impress.

The *fifth* period of Jewish history begins with the day of Israel's faring forth from Spain, his second home, once more to seek an abiding place. In the search, the nation is scattered over the European lands—Holland, Germany, Poland, everywhere. It is the period of stagnation in the intellectual life of the Jews, the reaction from exuberant productiveness to lassitude and sterility—a period during which the woe inflicted by the outside world is ever on the increase, and the spirit of the nation lies crushed into impotence. It lasts until the middle of the eighteenth century, until Moses Mendelssohn inaugurates a new era by introducing the Jews into the intellectual life of Germany, and through it once more into the civilization of the world at large. The inspiration of this our *sixth* and last period has not yet expended its force, and the current of thought that will call forth its successor cannot be predicted.

He who enters upon the consideration of the history of Israel in the spirit of critical research, as one might study, for instance, the history of the Phœnicians, the Arabs, or the French, will find much that is incomprehensible and inexplicable. The fact is, —and it is conceded by cool, dispassionate, even hostile historians—that the history of the Jews is a history of miracles and enigmas. But the miracles and enigmas are explained by the course of the history: <small>Peculiarity of Jewish History</small>

the *history* is testimony to the truth of the *miracles!* The historical account remains a riddle only to him who scans it callously and phlegmatically; but he who considers it with the eye of faith, who approaches it mindful of the biblical injunction: "Put off thy shoes from off thy feet, for the place whereon thou standest is holy ground," sees every feature of the history clearly; before him the development of Israel lies as an open book, telling how he has risen from humble, obscure beginnings to a position of prime importance in the culture and evolution of mankind.

On a sunny day—so reports the first modern historian of the Jews—nomad tribes entered the land of Canaan; they were our ancestors. We open the first books of the Bible, for in treating of the earliest period of Israel's history, we are in the fortunate position of having but to repeat an oft-told tale, whose incidents are part and parcel of our memory. Who is not familiar with the stories of the Bible? The Garden of Eden is disclosed to our view; we hear the serpent hiss; the rush of the waters of the deluge falls upon our ears; Noah's ark arises out of the abyss of destruction; with absorbed interest we follow the history of our patriarchs, the exemplars of our race.

Patriarchal History The father of our nation, Abraham, appears before our vision, sturdy and great, towering above his age. In a time in which men and beasts are offered as sacrifices everywhere, he understands God's summons to sacrifice his only son in the spirit, and so realizes that human sacrifices are never to be brought in Israel; that all the sacrifices current among the nations are to be eschewed in Israel. Then Isaac, the upright, appears, the provident father intent upon the well-being of his family, and Jacob with his sons, the little sheikh and his nomad tribe, journeying to Egypt, where the Israelites spread and multiply in the course of the centuries. We read the charming story of Joseph—its pathos brings tears to our eyes—and we marvel at the wondrous deliverance of the Israelites from Egyptian bondage. A small tribe of nomads they had entered, a great nation they departed, amid signs and wonders, pursued by Pharaoh, guided by divine Providence, and led by another spiritual giant, who towers not only above his own generation and age, but above all the generations and all the ages, the divinely inspired man Moses! What a figure! Not the art of Michael Angelo sufficed to body forth his heroic proportions. With three mountains his history is connected. On Horeb his mission originated; on Sinai it reached its culmination; on Nebo it was accomplished, and there Moses found his grave, yet "no man knoweth of his sepulchre unto this day." Through this man Moses Israel was made the recipient of divine revelation in the Law, which has been his guiding star during all his days. *[margin: Moses]*

In this Israelitish Law, three great cycles of thought are crystallized. By their application to life, Israelitish history develops into Jewish history, and Jewish history into the history of Christianity, or rather, into the *[margin: The Law]* history of human civilization. The Law holds in solution, first, the belief in one God; second, the belief, that He has proclaimed a moral law by which our life on earth must be regulated; and third, the belief, that all men are members of a great world-family of the future, foretold by divine promise; in other words, the belief in a Messiah, in the Messianic time.

These three lines of thought Mosaic legislation ushered into existence, and upon them rests the everlasting and universal value of Judaism, not to be depreciated by any amount of detraction.

Two peoples of antiquity originated, preserved, and transmitted to modern times all the treasures of humanity—the Hellenes and the Jews. Let us ask ourselves in all candor, what the character of human development would have been, if Greek culture alone with its continuation in Roman guise had moulded it. It admits of no doubt, that the Judaic spirit was indispensable to the symmetrical unfolding of the human mind. By how much tiny Israel surpassed his Hellenic contemporaries in ethical thought! Israel was the first to insist: "Thou shalt not kill!" The old chroniclers tell us that the Greek mountains often resounded with the cries of infants, and the waters of the Greek rivers often washed on shore the little children abandoned by their parents. To kill slaves was permissible; they were considered property, pure and simple, and no court, no authority could curtail the owner's right over them. Contrast with such views the Jewish attitude towards life and its responsibilities! With the ordinances of every festival the admonition is coupled: "Thou shalt hallow the feast, thou, thy manservant, thy maidservant, and thy stranger within thy gates." The most civilized nation of antiquity severely excludes strangers, whom it calls "barbarians"; the Israelitish Law enjoins: "Love thy neighbor as thyself"; or what is still more remarkable: "Love ye the stranger, for you have been strangers in the land of Egypt." Do not such principles raise the little Israelitish nation high above the Hellenes and other ancient disseminators of civilization, in fact, above the nations of later times? The triumph of our system of living lies in this, that modern dogmatism, in all its extent, has not gotten beyond *Shma' Israel*, the belief in one God, nor modern ethics, beyond *Weahavta le-Reakha kamokha*, "Love thy neighbor as thyself." A horde of day-laborers in brick and mortar were entrusted in the desert with the fundamentals of theology and morality, and as received by them they have come down to our day—miracle acknowledged alike by poet and by scientist. Herder says of it: "A history like this, with all its concomitant and dependent circumstances, cannot be a lying invention. Israel's Revelation, still incomplete, is the greatest miracle of all ages, and will continue until the last phase in the history of all the nations of the earth is reached." The importance of Israel, to be sure, has been misunderstood again and again. Men have not been able to conceive, how it was possible for a people only now escaped from the Egyptian taskmaster to become imbued with the idea of one God in a time characterized everywhere by polytheism. The *instinct* for monotheism was therefore invented and attributed to Israel. What a childish evasion, to give the name instinct to a sublime ethical idea, and to lodge it in one particular people, wanderers in the desert! The Greek Olympus was peopled with a multitude of gods. A plurality of gods cannot co-exist without discord and dissension. As mankind progressed, the gods were divided into male and female, but between the sexes, too, there is never-ending opposition. For Israel it was reserved to be the proclaimer of the belief in one God in a time given over to the worship of many gods. This belief was his salvation, his mission, his history.

Now he enters the Holy Land, and sojourns there nearly eight hundred years. Curiously, after the death of Moses, the account of Israel's progress is, on the whole, meagre and inadequate. We imagine a people devoted to the task of conquering the Promised Land from its inhabitants, zealous in expelling and exterminating its neighbors, deserting its God, and going after strange gods, rebelling against its leaders, and scorning the admonitions of its prophets. If this is all, the picture of the historical development of Israel in the early years of his existence as a nation is incomplete. From the moment Israel enters his old home, two currents can be traced: one political, one moral-religious. The political history is

Conquest of the Holy Land

free from all obscurity, yet we are filled with amazement at seeing Israel maintain his national strength as long as any people of antiquity. Neither Greeks, nor Assyrians, nor Romans had so long a period of national expansion. Modern Bible critics, who pluck the Bible to pieces with a wantonness that would not be tolerated in the study of Greek or Latin classical works, are far from agreed as to the time of the composition of Israel's most important poetic productions. Nearly all, however, unite in considering the Song of Deborah as the first blossom in the garden of Hebrew poetry. It is, indeed, worthy of note, that in this first Hebrew triumphal ode reference is made to the Revelation, the greatest miracle in history; in inspired measure the time is celebrated when the Lord went forth out of Seïr. Our point of view is different from that of the critics, but even if we granted theirs to be the correct one, we should, nevertheless, consider Deborah's mention of the Revelation on Sinai as a verification of the awesome event. As early as Deborah's days, we must infer, the Revelation was accepted, not only as an indisputable fact, but as an historical and religious event of the most far-reaching importance for Israel and humanity.

The time of the Judges is one of internal dissension and of violent struggles with the surrounding tribes. The end of the period is again signalized by the appearance of a remarkable figure, crowned with the aureole of poetry and enveloped in the splendor of history—

<small>The Kingdom</small>

Samuel the Priest. He is the last of the Judges and the inaugurator of the era in which kings rule Israel, a period of national glory, but at the same time one in which the religious idea is not maintained at the height to which it had been elevated by the generation blessed with the Revelation and by its successors. National self-consciousness attains its supreme development under David and Solomon. The erection of a central sanctuary in Jerusalem strengthens royal authority, and the foreign alliances negotiated by Solomon, his sagacity, his liberal, far-sighted policy, confer good repute upon Israel among the other nations. His prayer at the dedication of the Temple is one of the loftiest products of Jewish intellectual activity, the more remarkable as it belongs to a time in which many of the author's subjects inclined to idolatry, built altars, set up images, and neglected the service of the one God. From this time the above-mentioned double current becomes plainly visible: on the one hand, political power, now effectual, now paralyzed; on the other hand, the moral-religious current, controlled by the prophets, whose influence transcends by far the boundaries of their time.

The prophets have been called "divine demagogues" by the modern writer Renan —they have been likened to the modern socialists and revolutionary leaders. The comparison may appear irreverent, but it is seen not to be destitute of truth, when one remembers that they ventured to chide a people, the greater part of

The Prophets

which had invited destruction by iniquitous and impious conduct—a people, rebellious not only against the prophets, but against its kings and its God! In such days the divinely-inspired men stepped forth, and taught Israel how far he had departed from the path of rectitude, how disloyal he had become to the noble ideals of his faith. With equal manliness and courage they rebuked the other nations, holding up to each the mirror of correction and repentance. Still more! In that age of relentless struggle—an age in which the old Greeks were busy investing the gods of their Olympus with intensely human attributes—the prophets arose and proclaimed to mankind the belief in a new time, to be realized perhaps in a far-off future, when all nations "shall beat their swords into ploughshares," when war shall cease from off the earth, and men shall recognize, that in heaven above there is but one God, the Ruler of the universe, and here below but one brotherhood of united mankind. Such a vision in such times! In all human history, in the whole process of the evolution of spiritual life, no analogy can be found to the Hebrew prophets. It is incomprehensible how one can hope to explain, by the circumstances of their time, the nature of men who considered themselves specially called and empowered to execute a high mission, to spread abroad the idea, that the day will come when but one religion will prevail on earth, which not even in our days, perhaps least of all in our days, would meet with acceptance. This is the idea to be borne in mind.

For to know the history of a people, it is not necessary to be acquainted with all its names and numbers, its kings and princes, its prophets and poets. The fundamental idea must be grasped and remembered: In the desert Israel was made the recipient of a Revelation teaching belief in the one God, forbidding murder, and enjoining love of one's neighbors, though they be aliens in tongue and faith. Israel was made the bearer of a Law that to this day appears as the remote, unattainable, ideal goal of the moral and civil development of man, prohibiting, as it does, usury and the taking of interest, and preventing the concentration of vast riches and property. Five hundred years later the prophets proclaimed the belief in a noble future, in which the whole world will worship one God; in which humanity, faith, religious conviction, will be one and inseparable.

These three basic thoughts must be digested to understand the history of Israel, to comprehend his preservation in the face of a world of enemies.

What the development of Jewish life would have been, had the prophets not thundered their admonitions at a people standing on the brink of destruction, is idle speculation. It is enough for us to know that clear-eyed they discerned impending ruin, and warned Israel by painting the picture of his persecutors.

Israel, however, continued in the path he had chosen. The two realms separated, and Israel, the kingdom of northern Palestine, appealed to the enemy to compose internal differences. Shalmaneser, the Assyrian, came with a host, and he came not to help the kings of Israel, but to annihilate the kingdom of Israel, the kingdom of the Ten Tribes. That happened in the year 720 before the common era. **The Ten Tribes** It is remarkable and perhaps one of the profoundest mysteries of the Jewish past, that the Ten Tribes never reappear in history. In the Talmud we are told that the remnants of the Ten Tribes were scattered, and are to be sought for here and there, but no one has ever found, and probably no one ever will find, a visible trace of them. Judah, the possessor of Jerusalem, maintained itself for about two centuries, until 587, until the mighty conqueror Nebuchadnezzar, the Babylonian, overran it, and Jerusalem and the Temple suffered their first destruction. **Destruction of the First Temple**

With this catastrophe the first period of Jewish historical development closes. On the ruins of the Temple sits Jeremiah, one of the loftiest of Israel's prophets, and when we read his Lamentations to-day, we feel as though he were addressing them not only to the crushed Israelites, his contemporaries, but to the Israel of our time. "What shall I compare unto thee, O daughter of Jerusalem? what shall I find equal to thee, that I may comfort thee, O virgin daughter of Zion? for great like the sea is thy breach; who can bring healing to thee?" "Oh! how doth she sit solitary—the city that was full of people is become like a widow! she that was so great among the nations, the princess among the provinces, is become tributary!"

So the prophet laments, and consolation he finds nowhere. Jeremiah goes into exile with his people, and even in the bitterness of banishment he continues to affirm the belief, that better days are in store for his poor Israel. Another prophet, Ezekiel, joins the exiles, and as they journey through Ramah a voice is heard groaning and weeping. Far as the eye can reach, no human being can be discerned; it is a ghostly voice, the voice of Rachel, the mother in Israel, weeping for her children and refusing to be comforted. Then, like a whisper from heavenly heights, they hear the soothing words: "Refrain thy voice from weeping, and thy eyes from tears; for there is a reward for thy work, saith the Lord, and they shall return from the land of the enemy!" *And they did return!*

II

As so often in the subsequent history of the Jews, we hear at the close of the first period the bitter lament: Our hope is put to shame, our enemies have ravaged us, our Temple is dismantled, our God has abandoned us—all is over! This is the plaintive strain resounding again and again in the history of Israel, but no less do we hear accents of joy, when the situation changes. And the change never failed to come. If history is read with intelligent attention, with a philosopher's eye, a different idea of it can be derived from that to be gathered from a mere compilation of names and dates, wars, victories, and revolutions. History has no worth unless we abstract from it a practical application, a moral. We shall gain the moral of Jewish history by and by. If it does not obtrude itself in the course of our presentation of the subject, it will prove that we have fallen short of clearness and precision.

The hope of the Jews, then, was utterly quenched. They went into captivity with nothing to secure their solidarity: their home was given over to the stranger, the relentless enemy had driven them forth into distant lands. *The Captivity* But lo!—was it one of the whimseys of chance, was it the first harbinger of the wondrous fate that was to preside over the Jews' whole history?—their very conqueror Nebuchadnezzar proves to be a gracious monarch unto them in their exile lands, his very people are favorably inclined to the forlorn sojourners. They are put upon a footing of equality with his other subjects; they build houses, they cultivate fields. In short, scarcely fifty years elapsed, and they were looked upon as acceptable, respected citizens of the land they had entered a mob of captives. In the half century, to be sure, they had had to suffer the caprice of successive monarchs. After Nebuchadnezzar came his son, who was not so kindly disposed towards them. Then the violent wars broke out that were to precipitate the Babylonian empire from the height of its puissance into destruction. The legend of King Cyrus is well-known: how he with his troops in one night captured the beleaguered capital, killed the king, and united the realm with his own. Now golden days dawned for the Jews. It is held, that Cyrus knew their religion, and was therefore filled with friendly intentions towards them. It certainly is true, that he poured out upon them the abundance of his kindness, and even granted them permission to return to their country. With indescribable jubilation the news was received, though not all availed themselves of the precious privilege of going back. Fifty years after their banishment, forty-two thousand Jews journeyed homeward from Babylon, singing psalms, as tradition has it, with the recurring refrain: Happy the nation whose protector is Jehovah, who has helped it, and led it forth out of the land of the enemy! The word was fulfilled: "When the Lord bringeth

The Return

back again the captivity of Zion, ... then shall our mouth be filled with laughter, and our tongue with singing." The returning exiles set out on their homeward journey, accompanied by the ardent blessings and loaded down with the gifts and treasures for the rebuilding of the Temple showered upon them by their brethren who remained behind. They had so intimately identified themselves with their Babylonian neighbors, that they could not endure the idea of uprooting and transplanting themselves.

Exaltation and jubilant rejoicing were followed by their natural revulsion, a time of disappointment, weary discouragement, and listlessness. As no traveller has yet gone to the Holy Land to satisfy the sad-hued yearning of his heart for a sight of the spots hallowed by patriarchs and prophets without suffering acute disenchantment; so the exiles, expecting to take possession of the Promised Land, according to the poetical description, flowing with milk and honey, inherited devastation and desolation. The Temple was a ruin; the place on which it had stood was strewn with its debris. There was nothing for it but to begin at the very beginning. The work of restoration was all the harder, as they had but one hand free to employ in building; the other wielded the sword against their enemies. Foremost among them was a mixed populace of older residents, called Samaritans. They at first met the Jews with friendly advances, and offered assistance in the erection of the Temple. Knowing what

The Samaritans

to expect from such false friends, the Jews rebuffed them. In revenge, the Samaritans, under the leadership of Manasseh, the son of a priest, erected a Temple on Gerizim, designed to be the competitor and rival of the sanctuary in Jerusalem. It was not the last time that the Samaritans made the life of the Jews miserable. It is characteristic of the religious life shaped by Judaism, that its dissenting sects either perished at birth, or never got beyond a sort of galvanized existence. The Samaritans have maintained a semblance of life up to this day. Only a short while ago a letter of the Samaritan high priest fell into my hands, in which he complains, that the Jews still regard his nation as their enemy, and spread the report that it worships a dove. In all, he says, the Samaritans count one hundred and twenty families, who are so poor that they depend upon alms. This precisely, as we shall see in the course of our presentation, is the history of the other sects that time and again separated themselves from the body of the Jews.

Meanwhile hopeless discouragement seized upon the Jews. "The stars in their courses" battled against them: hail and other untoward phenomena destroyed their seedling crops, and their harvest yield was small and wretched. In vain the last prophets, Haggai and Zachariah, tried to rouse their energies. Again, with the abruptness of a miracle, an event occurred, apparently incapable of explanation, which was to effect a complete transformation in the situation of the Jews of the Holy Land. One day a priest from Babylon arrived in

Jerusalem and with him a goodly company of priests, Levites, Nethinim, and Israelites. He came fortified with a letter from the king of Persia, and freighted with the free-will offerings of his brethren, who, though living in the land of exile, never "forgot Jerusalem." The priest was Ezra, "a ready scribe in the Law of Moses," and justly called the "second Moses" by posterity. From him the second great period of the history of Judaism dates. Of wide vision, of exalted conception of life, fearless and courageous, pure of heart, and strenuous in action, he was in every respect fashioned to be the reformer of his people. After he had settled in Jerusalem, his first work was directed towards the correction of a widely prevalent abuse. In their degenerateness, shepherdless as they were,—their first leader Zerubbabel had not been strong enough—the Jews had intermingled with the heathen. Jews had married heathen women, who had introduced them to the vices of the heathen nations. Ezra assembled the whole people on a Feast, and read them the Law, emphasizing the passages in which marriage with the heathen is rigorously forbidden. The reading of the Law aroused astonishment in those days. Eighty years had passed since the return of the Israelites from Babylon; they had forgotten all they had known of the Law; of the prohibition to intermarry with the heathen they were completely ignorant. The people murmured. But Ezra knew when to employ unmitigated severity. The heathen women were excluded from the circle of the Jews, the building of the sanctuary was energetically resumed, and in the year 516, eight hundred years after the redemption from Egyptian servitude, the second Temple was consecrated. Among the participants in the solemn service were some that had seen the first House. They wept bitterly, for the splendor of the first sanctuary was unattainable. Yet, despite their repining, it had to be conceded, that the prophecy had been fulfilled: the glory of the first Temple had been renewed. Sorry and insignificant as it was, the Temple had been toilsomely rebuilt by a handful of people with their scanty hoardings. They had a national sanctuary, a centre about which they could rally.

The Second Temple

Fourteen years later a man of equally heroic stature, **Nehemiah**, came from the East to Jerusalem, likewise bearing costly gifts and accompanied by brave warriors. These two leaders together, Ezra and Nehemiah, set about a great and laborious undertaking, the reformation of Judaism. The time of Ezra and Nehemiah is wrapped in profound darkness. We are much better informed about the period preceding it than about the time of Ezra and his successors, who were called the *Soferim*, Scribes, not, of course, to be taken in the modern sense of the word. But we know that they accomplished a precious, imperishable work: they set down in writing the Pentateuch, thus rescuing it from oblivion for all future generations, for the whole world. Many refuse to believe that

Nehemiah

The Scribes

the Bible was composed as it has been transmitted to us, and that, as we assume, the Five Books of Moses were written by Moses, the Book of Joshua, by Joshua, etc. Most German critics maintain, that the essential parts of the Law were composed by Ezra and his co-laborers, the *Soferim*. The reproach necessarily incurred by these critics, that they brand our pious fathers as forgers, as cunning priests, they cast off from themselves by every manner of effort to justify their views. They hold that Ezra put the Law together out of the remnants of folk tales and popular conceptions. We cannot here pursue this subject further. He who reads the Five Books of Moses, I do not say with the eyes of faith, but with unbiased, unclouded mind, must at once recognize the futility of such criticism. Has nation ever been heard of that would allow a solitary priest suddenly to impose upon it a legal code like that prescribed in the Mosaic Law? We believe, and shall hold fast to the conviction, that Ezra, on the Feast of Tabernacles, read to the Israelites the Five Books of Moses, which had fallen into oblivion, and that all the men and women, the hoary and the young, took upon themselves anew the obligation to regulate their lives according to the mandates of the inherited Law.

Another report from those remote days meets with incredulity, that then and later a synod existed called the "Men of the Great Assembly," whose task was, on the one hand the adaptation of tradition to new circumstances, on the other, the preservation of the old traditions in their purity. This great synod, modern critics say, never existed. But whatever their opinion, the Men of the Great Assembly were the conservators of tradition. If there had not been such men as we imagine the leaders of the Great Assembly to have been, the myth-shaping fancy of the people would have had to create them in order to arrive at a natural explanation for the preservation of the body of tradition.

The Great Assembly

For about two hundred years the Israelites lived peacefully under Persian and Median rulers, until one day a great event again stirred Israel mightily. The hero was the prince that deserves perhaps to be called the greatest of antiquity, Alexander the Great. On his triumphal march through the world he did not pass Jerusalem by. He had gone as far as India in his conquering progress, and now he was advancing with a mighty army against tiny Jerusalem. No doubt the city will fall a prey to his power, and Israel is on the verge of destruction. Dressed in flowing robes, and followed by a retinue of pious priests, the high priest goes out to meet the warrior. The priests are the bearers of gifts to the hero; they open the gates of the Holy City, and entreat his mercy. And lo! the world-conquering Alexander assures them of his gracious inclination towards them, and that he had had no thought of attempting the capture of Jerusalem. The appearance of the high priest has so overwhelmed him that his attendants cannot account

Alexander the Great

for his emotion. The story is told, that in the desert Alexander was visited by a dream, in which he was shown the high priest as he now met him, interceding for his land and people. And though he subdues all other lands, he spares Jerusalem, and with his army withdraws from Palestine. He gives the Jews assurance of his favor, and promises them protection against their oppressors.

Unfortunately, the empire established by him was of short duration; lands so widely separated could not be brought under one sceptre permanently. His realm was divided up under his immediate successors, and the Israelites again became the prey of strange nations. The Egyptians possessed themselves of their land and its defenseless inhabitants. Ptolemy Lagi likewise was favorably inclined towards the Jews, and many of them were taken by him to his own land. Eleven thousand Jews were settled in Egypt in this way, and their migration marks the beginning of a tremendous movement within Judaism. A fraction of the race had remained in Babylonia, the kernel was in Jerusalem, and now another fragment, not by any means the most despicable element, left the mother country and settled in Alexandria, the most influential centre of culture in the old world. The Jewish colony in Alexandria was scarcely a hundred years old—and this is characteristic of the intellectual aspirations and endowments of the Jewish people—when the Jews wrote Greek as well as, in part better than, the Greeks themselves. They even composed Greek

Alexandrian Jews

verse, so perfect that they could venture to attribute it to Sophocles. At that time a little Jew was wont to pass through the streets of Alexandria to the museum. When he opened the door, silence fell upon all within. It was Philo the Jew, who, the Greeks admitted, wrote Greek as well as Plato, the classic ideal of Greek literature. The Jews were authors, philosophers, actors, merchant princes, and all this less than a century after entering Egypt as aliens. Here for the first time in the history of mankind Jew met Greek, the two chief promoters of ancient civilization, whose achievements for the preservation of science are greater than those of all other nations. The first contact between them, at least in Alexandria, was cordial. The Jew Philo was the founder of the Neoplatonic philosophy, concerning which I shall mention only the one fact, that it became the basis of the Church philosophy of the middle ages. Moreover, from his philosophy taken in connection with the ideas of the prophets, the shoot sprouted forth that was destined to develop into a spreading tree, for in part Philo's philosophy is the basis of Christianity.

Not quite so genial was the meeting of Jew and Greek at home, in Jerusalem, where a characteristic trait displayed itself, which, under changed conditions, may be observed to this day: The rich Jews knew no dearer aim, cherished no more ardent desire, than to have their Judaism sink into the background and be forgotten, and to mix with the Greeks, assume Greek names, imitate Greek depravity and vices,

The Hellenists

and frequent the palaces, the palestra, gymnasium, circus, and theatre of the Greeks. The line in Lessing's "Nathan the Wise": "The rich Jew I never esteemed the better Jew," is matched by a remarkable Talmudic utterance: "Have a jealous care of the children of the poor, for from them goes forth the Law." The rich Jews have never done anything to save Judaism. It is impossible to calculate what the course of Jewish development would have been, had the rich of Hellenistic days, supported by the aristocratic priesthood, carried out their ideas, and had Judaism not boasted a small circle of men, who, though giving the due meed of admiration to the lofty and beautiful features in Greek art and poetry, preserved their faith intact in all its purity. This chosen band consisted of the staunch rabbis, who developed the fundamental principles of Judaism in the Talmud, the work well known by name at least.

The conflict raged between the hostile factions, the Sadducees, composed of the priests and aristocrats, and the Pharisees, consisting of the doctors of the Law, until a foreign conqueror, Antiochus Epiphanes, entered the unhappy land, and once more, in 169, subjected it to foreign domination. He determined to make the Jews feel what a strong ruler is capable of doing. Not satisfied with having subdued the land, he wounded the Jews in their most sensitive spot: he forbade them to pay obedience to the injunctions of the Law, and desecrated the

Antiochus Epiphanes

Temple by setting up a statue of the Olympian Jupiter within its precincts. City after city in Palestine was defiled in the same way. Modin, the little highland town, was not spared. An old Jewish priest lived there, by name Mattathias. He had never been in sympathy with the doings in the capital. The aping of strange customs had been a thorn in his side. He dared stand up and refuse to sacrifice to Jupiter. Another priest proved more docile, and Mattathias slew him by the altar smoking from the offering brought to the heathen deity. That was the signal for a general uprising. Mattathias and his five sons organized the rebellion, and, like wildfire, the report spread, that a priestly family of Modin had had the courage to bid defiance to the conqueror. His valiant countrymen dispersed here and there gathered under his banner, and a small troop of five thousand men, unarmed or inadequately equipped, they ranged themselves on the plain of Emmaus, under the leadership of Judas Maccabæus, Mattathias' son, opposite to an army of fifty thousand infantry and ten thousand cavalry, veterans who had subdued the most warlike peoples. Yet the little band routed the great host. The story of Emmaus repeated itself again and again. Barely two years later, Judas Maccabæus, with an army of ten thousand, put to flight the Syrian host numbering sixteen thousand infantry and four thousand riders. In triumph he journeyed to Jerusalem, purified the Temple, and on the twenty-fifth day of Kislew, 165, the sanctuary was rededicated

The Maccabees

to its pristine purpose, the service of the one God. In commemoration of the event we celebrate the Chanukkah festival.

A wealth of wonders and legends, of tales and narratives, of heroes and martyrs, mark the time of the Syrian wars, proving anew, that faith, though it live in a small, weak nation, can accomplish miracles and heroic deeds. Judas the Maccabean perished like a hero on the battlefield, and his brothers John and Simon assumed the leadership. During the next hundred years, the Israelites lived by turns under the rule of heroes and of cowards. The Maccabean race did not always maintain itself upon the heights of moral and physical heroism. The third generation, John Hyrcanus and Aristobulus, had sunk into such pusillanimity, that they summoned the foe to help against their own brothers. This new foe, another conqueror, mightier than any since Alexander the Great, was the Roman nation. Even then a world-power, it was the political authority before which the world, the old and the new, trembled; the victor who knew how to annihilate all nations and counteract all military art by crafty politics. Pompey entered Jerusalem, but the aim of the cowardly princes that had invited him thither was not realized; the Romans turned Palestine into a Roman province. Though under Emperor Augustus the Jews were considered citizens, still they were dependent upon Rome, and obliged to pay her a tribute. The rulers of the Idumæan house, among them Herod the Great, multiplied the evils of the

The Romans in Palestine

3

situation. Fifty years after the heroic devotion of the Maccabees, not a trace of the old patriotism, the old loyalty to the faith, could be found. The men whom we venerate to-day as the preservers of Judaism had to hide themselves in mountain caves, and as for Herod's savagery, we know that he had ten wives, and that he ordered the execution of three of his sons, of his brother-in-law, his brother-in-law's mother, and thousands of others.

Herod died in the year 4 before the common era. Three years before his death a son named Joshua had been born to the carpenter Joseph in Nazareth. He was destined to wield extraordinary influence over the fate of the Jewish people, in fact, over that of the whole world. But it would be false to suppose that the influence was operative in the time we are speaking of, or soon after.

<small>Jesus of Nazareth</small>

The situation of the Jews in Jerusalem at about the beginning of the present era was most wretched. Internal dissension had divided the people into hostile camps. The aristocratic and the rich were arrayed against the priests and the poor. The news of the state of affairs in Jerusalem had spread to the provinces, and reached the fishermen of Galilee. Then probably the idea of bringing help to his people flashed into the lofty, enthusiastic mind of Joshua. It was not his intention to change Judaism; he wanted to infuse new life into the sick body of the Jewish people; he wanted to unite the hostile parties; he wanted to become the reformer of his people. He walked in the ways of Hillel, whose teaching lay before him, and what he proclaimed on the public street to a people that did not understand him was practically the same that his teacher had inculcated a hundred years earlier. When one of the Gentiles came to the latter, and begged to have the whole of the Jewish Law imparted to him while standing on one foot, Hillel answered: "Certainly; love thy neighbor as thyself. That is the whole of Judaism." Eighty years later Rabbi Joshua repeated the saying, and, if the speeches reported in the Gospels are genuine, he added, "On this hangeth the whole Law." Assuredly, he was a pious rabbi, and unnoticed flowed on the life of him who had conceived the sublime idea of reforming Israel. Even the rabbis mocked at him, for not like them was he learned in the Law. For about a year he proclaimed the redemption of the world by the Messiah, which, the prophets had foretold, would come to pass in a time in which confusion and affliction were at their height. In Jerusalem Roman procurators were stationed, and one day Pontius Pilate was informed, that a man was going up and down in the land preaching revolution against Rome, and teaching that temporal power no longer had any justification. Pontius Pilate reported the facts to the highest court, the Synhedrion, and the man was summoned to Jerusalem. All sorts of people now joined him, and his progress to the city in a measure was a triumphal procession. The scene is familiar to all, how, when Joshua of Nazareth stood before the Synhedrion, and Pilate asked the question: "Art thou the king of the Jews?" he answered: "Thou sayest it." From this it appears, that the great thought must have come to him before, that he himself was called to be the Messiah of his people. Pontius Pilate recognized the danger to Rome, and charged the Synhedrion to pass judgment upon him. He was nailed to the cross—a form of execution never used by the Jews. Among all the kinds of punishment prescribed by the Synhedrion, that of death by crucifixion is not to be found.

Golgotha, the place of skulls, gave birth to a tragedy in which the Israelitish people was assigned a calamitous part. Joshua ha-Nozri developed into Jesus Christ, whose successors, the apostles, founded a religion based upon Judaism. Not only did they later use every effort to separate the new faith from the old, but again and again they took hostile measures against the mother religion. When it occurred, the portentous event seems to have been passed over in silence. The only authors of the period, Philo and Josephus, make no mention of Jesus the Messiah. In his generation, therefore, either no attention was paid to him, or he was regarded as one of the pious prophets, such as probably arose in numbers in the Jerusalem of his day.

Soon afterwards, another tragedy, no less awful and sublime, was enacted upon the soil of the Holy Land: the siege of Jerusalem and the destruction of the Temple! The city had long been a prey to bitter factional strife, when Titus in the year 70 appeared before its walls with a powerful army.

Then began a life and death struggle, the more disastrous as not even to the enemy the inhabitants of the city presented a united front. The various parties—the rich and the aristocratic priests (Sadducees), the doctors of the Law (Pharisees), the military leaders and the Zealots (Kanaim), in short, all the parties that had been at feud with each other since generations, or had sprung up during the siege—even now pursued their peculiar aims and interests. The numbers involved in the conflict and its entire history are amazing. The captives ran up to about ninety-seven thousand; in the neighborhood of twelve thousand died of starvation during the siege, and the whole number of the victims of the war is computed at one million one hundred thousand. On the Ninth of Ab the Romans cast a firebrand into one of the buildings adjacent to the north side of the Temple. With the fury of lightning the flames spread, and the Romans penetrated into the Temple. Soon the whole mount was a great sea of fire, and the howls of triumph issuing from the victorious Romans mingled in curious harmony with the lamentations of the defeated Jews. In the last chamber of the Temple, six thousand unarmed men, who had sought refuge there, were burnt.

<small>Destruction of Jerusalem by Titus</small>

The victors did not escape without serious losses. The walls and fortifications of the city and the stubborn opposition of its inhabitants had put their strength to the severest test. Had it not been for the old hereditary fault, disunion among the Jews, who knows how long the army of Vespasian and Titus might have had to stand before the walls of Jerusalem! Of the factions at odds with each other, the Zealots had been the ones to insist upon the continuation of the war until all means were exhausted; the others had been willing to surrender in order to secure mild conditions of peace. So Jerusalem finally became the prey of the Romans.

A remarkable narrative has come down to us in connection with the catastrophe. When the last high priest, standing upon the summit of the Temple Mount, saw the legions of Titus rush up the hill to the sanctuary of the Lord, realizing that the end had come unto Israel and his House, he took the golden keys that unlocked the Temple, and held them up into the clouds. A hand stretched forth from out of the clouds, and grasped the keys. This is a legend. But what was in the minds of the men who preserved the legend in the Talmud? They meant to indicate, that Israel's mission had undergone a transformation; it was no longer linked with the Temple and the land of the fathers. His task was now to become what his prophets had proclaimed: a witness before the nations of the belief in the one God and the eternal law of morality revealed on Sinai—a witness unto the truths of Judaism.

Now the miraculous occurs! A nation journeys forth out of its home, and carries naught with it—not a grain of the dust of the Holy Land, not a pebble to bear testimony to the glory of the Temple—only a book, a single book, its Bible, which had been its refuge and tower of strength in happy days. It wanders on, across blood, in the midst of nations, through tears, and over thrones, the might of tyrants and the treachery of hosts of enemies encompassing it, always holding aloft the Book. The Book supports the people, and braves its fate. So it passes out of the Holy Land in quest of a new home.

III

ONCE more my readers must transport themselves to Jerusalem the old, the soil on which the most stirring events of our national history have taken place. In the bloody days in which many thousands of Jews met death, and the remnant of the people went into exile, an event took place which at the time probably aroused no notice, but which has turned out to have been of determining influence in the development of Judaism. Through the streets of Zion, the beleaguered city, a funeral cortege is moving. Disciples are carrying a beloved teacher to the grave. The procession is permitted to pass unhindered, for even the Roman guards refrain from putting an indignity upon a corpse, and so the bier is borne through the very city gates unchallenged. The company has scarcely gotten beyond the walls of the Jerusalem of raging Zealots and despairing peace partisans, when the bearers set down their burden, and raise the lid of the coffin. Out of it steps an old rabbi: Rabbi Jochanan ben Zakkai. To execute his plan he had been forced to resort to this subterfuge in order to get outside of the city, closely invested by the Romans. At the head of his band of disciples, he proceeds to the enemy's camp, and presents himself before the Roman commander, Vespasian.

Jochanan ben Zakkai

Impressed by the venerable rabbi's appearance,

the general pays heed to him, and being in a good humor permits him to prefer a petition. What is the rabbi's prayer? He asks neither that Jerusalem be spared, nor that the Temple be protected, nor that his own family be exempted from harm. His one request of the proud Roman emperor is: "Let me found a school at Jabne." Astonished and not a little contemptuous, the Roman looks at the Jew who has no other wish at such a time; yet he nods gracious assent. At the head of his disciples, Jochanan journeys to Jabne, a little town by the sea, about thirty miles from Jerusalem. The scornful Roman little suspects that Greek museums, the pyramids of Egypt, the temples of Rome, and the impregnable castles of mediæval knights will have crumbled into dust and ashes, when the Law of Jochanan, issuing from Jabne to every corner of the earth, will still exist with vitality undiminished.

Jochanan discerned clearly, that a new era had dawned with changed demands; that Israel thenceforth would have larger tasks to fulfil. In a time in which it seemed that the curse foretelling Israel's ruin had been realized, he gathered all available forces to Jabne. He inculcated the idea that the sacrificial cult would have to be abandoned, that prayer would have to be substituted for sacrifice, that the Jews had the new mission to go out among men, among the nations, to proclaim the belief in one God. Jabne gave the impetus to a reorganization of Judaism. Without being either prince or priest, Jochanan, by reason of his intellect, his knowledge, his example, exerted a stimulating and vivifying influence upon his disciples and upon the fragments of his dispersed people. Gamaliel was his true successor in the spirit, the first of a line of masters animated by similar ideals and gifted with equal force. One of the most enlightened of them and at the same time one of the most pious is the teacher whose name, Akiba, has a familiar ring in the ear of every Jew.

<small>Akiba</small>

He, too, considered Israel's mission a spiritual one, but the conviction did not prevent him from pursuing another aim and cherishing another ideal. Jochanan had buried Jerusalem under her own ruins, but Akiba did not resign the hope of political and national regeneration. He fondly believed that it might still be possible to rebuild the Temple, and he became a great political agitator. The essential facts of his career, to be sure, have not reached our day. Up to his fortieth year he is said to have been employed by a wealthy Jew as cowherd. His rich employer's daughter, the story goes, fell in love with him, but her father would not accept him as his son-in-law. Thereupon Akiba journeyed to Babylon, and so earnestly devoted himself to study that he returned at the end of a few years a famous master, to whom Kalba Sebua gladly gave his daughter, for she had remained faithful to her lover.

Akiba undertook extensive journeys in the interest of his political plans. On one of them he met a man whose wonderful beauty and well-proportioned, strong frame attracted him. As if lost in a dream, he looked at him long, and finally exclaimed: "A star has risen in Jacob! Thou wilt be the deliverer, thou wilt be the Messiah." The man thus apostrophized was Bar-Kokhba, to whom Akiba paid homage as the new king. Bar-Kokhba did not disappoint the hopes of his admirers. He gathered a great army, and entrenched himself in the rock-fortress Bethar, the centre of another forlorn struggle against Roman supremacy, more relentless than any that Rome herself had ever engaged in. Its luridness makes even the siege of Jerusalem sink into the background.

<small>Bar-Kokhba</small>

For three years the haughty Romans were kept before the walls of Bethar, and even then, it is said, the fortress fell through treachery. The old hereditary enemies of the Jews, the Samaritans, betrayed to the alien foe the secret of unguarded entrances. On a Sabbath the Romans poured in through the unprotected passages, and Bar-Kokhba himself probably met his death in the desperate struggle that ensued, for we hear nothing more about him. The strength of the nation was laid low forever, and Jerusalem ordered to be turned into a ploughed field. On the Ninth of Ab, the anniversary of its two destructions, a ploughshare was drawn over the site of the Temple, and later a sanctuary sacred to Jupiter was erected on it. The very name of Jerusalem was to be obliterated; the place was to be known as ÆLIA CAPITOLINA. Rabbi Akiba was the most distinguished object of Hadrian's revenge. He and seven others, or, as the legend goes, ten martyrs, were executed in an open square, having first been subjected to the most exquisite tortures. Before his soul left its body, Akiba pronounced the confession of faith: "Hear, O Israel, the Lord is our God, the Lord is One!" So he died, but the spirit that has maintained Israel by no means died with him. It merely transplanted itself to another soil. In Babylonia, in fact, it attained to greater strength then ever in Jerusalem. The narrowly national history of Israel closes with the tragedy of Bethar, the favorite subject of epics, ballads, and dramas. Henceforth Israel's history is a history of his suffering and his persecutions. It no longer concentrates itself upon the soil of one country, for Israel becomes a wanderer to the "four corners of the earth," in all the habitations of men.

In reality, the history of the Jews from that time on is the history of their literature; they preserve themselves by means of their intellectual activity, exercised upon the text-book of their life, the Bible. The Bible is the native home of the Jew. Without it he would have drifted anchorless; with it every place was home, a refuge hospitably open for his reception.

This mental activity of the Jews, absorbing their every force and faculty during a period of hundreds of years, built up the colossal monument called the Talmud, the precipitate of the work of centuries, representing the devoted effort of generations of Jews, under the direction of the most eminent masters, especially

The Talmud

of those in Babylonia, where the Jews, enjoying social respect, were permitted to lead a free, unrestrained life.

Until the year 500 of the present era, the centre of gravity of Judaism lay in Babylonia. But before that time, the Jews had wandered far and wide. We know that they had settled in Germany. We hear of a Jewish bishop of Metz, Simon by name. At the end of the third century we read of a Jewish congregation at Cologne, and at the same time a number of Jewish settlements were established at other places along the Rhine. Evidence is not lacking, that the Jews reached the Rhine before the Teutons, who so often, down to our own day, have disputed the claim of the former to German citizenship equal to their own. And we hear of great Jewish kingdoms at the "opposite ends" of the earth, in southern and northern Arabia. Powerful kings reigned there, who by some chance or other obtained supremacy over all the highland tribes, and the conquered accepted Judaism with their rulers. Likewise we hear of Jews at that early time settled in Spain, and of some in central Arabia. *The Diaspora*

In central Arabia they were so highly considered, that when one day in Mecca, a man arose, full of the desire to systematize and fix in permanent form the disjointed ideas upon religion held by the Arabs, he sought to enter into relations first with the Jews of Mecca, then with those of Medina. Finding that the Jews turn towards the East in their synagogues, he advised his race-brethren to do the same. The man was Mohammed. He tried to win the Jews over to his ideas. He was as cunning as fanatic, and the Jews of the city were on their guard against him. With the expenditure of all their strength, they had succeeded in preserving their faith, and they had no wish to sacrifice it for the vagaries of the fanatic enthusiast. Some, however, became his followers. Every one knows what success attended the propaganda of his fanatic, extravagant conception of life, appealing peculiarly to the fancy and the prejudices of the Arabs. He was the founder of Islam.

<small>Mohammed</small>

The Jews had made themselves part and parcel of Arab life. The Jewish contemporaries of Mohammed wrote and composed poetry in Arabic as good as the Greek of the Alexandrian Jews eight hundred years earlier; or as the Aramaic of the Babylonian Jews eight hundred years before the Alexandrians; or as the Hebrew of the Palestinian Jews eight hundred years before the Babylonians. Here we meet with one of the chief factors in the success of the Jews as agents of civilization. Wherever they went, be it to the edge of the desert or into Teutonic lands, they founded first, not synagogues or houses of prayer, but schools, for they knew, that what alone had saved them, dispersed as they were in exile lands, was the spirit that came forth out of the houses of learning. "On the breath issuing from the schools rests the moral order of the universe," says the Talmud.

<small>The Arabian Jews</small>

The development of the Islam proceeded with mighty strides, and its influence extended far and wide over the whole Eastern world. When the Arabs sat in their tents in the fair summer twilight, we can imagine them telling the legend of a man who was the exemplar of hospitality and bravery. His name was Samuel ben Adijah, and by race he was a Jew—so respected the Jews were shortly after they had made their first permanent settlement in Arabia. Among the poems in praise of courage and ·guestfriendship that have come down to us from before the time of Mohammed, the favorite one cited by the Arabs was Samuel's *Kasside*. Even among those who spread Mohammed's doctrines there were Jewish authors and authoresses, some of whose clever epigrams and poems have been preserved to this day. They are so thoroughly permeated with the spirit of free Arabia, that if their successors had not informed us of the facts of their lives, we should never have suspected the writers to be Jews.

All this was to change. When Mohammed perceived, that the Jews were not accepting his leadership, he ceased to court their favor, and after a while he began to persecute them. He wrote the twenty-ninth Sura in the Koran, directed against the Jews, and forbade his adherents to turn towards the East in prayer.

Israel once more had to experience the antagonism of a daughter religion. As soon as the Roman world-empire had fallen, and Christianity had attained to independent power, the crescent and the cross united to attack and oppress Israel. Perhaps this was poor policy on Mohammed's part. Christianity was true to itself in pursuing the policy. Its very existence rested upon the proposition that it was the sole vehicle of the truth. If this claim was to appear tenable, no Jew could be permitted to live, for he would testify against its validity. The most insignificant, the most despised Jew is a loud witness against Christianity, and therefore he must be wiped from the face of the earth.

The first emperors that professed Christianity followed this course. Constantine was the only one to honor the custom of Jew-persecuting more in the breach than the observance. Julian the Apostate once more dreamed the unrealizable dream of the rebuilding of Jerusalem. He informed the Jews of his plan, but soon his attempt was abandoned. The other emperors, like their German successors, and like the Spanish kings and the Visigothic rulers, looked towards the one goal, harbored the one wish, to exterminate the Jews.

They failed, for the stiffnecked Jews were animated by a spiritual force incapable of being crushed. If the Jews had remained a political entity, they would doubtless have succumbed to the assault of the combined powers of the world. As it was, what could the Jews be robbed of? Their spiritual possessions were inalienable. From the ashes of every pyre rose in renewed vigor the Jewish spirit, or, as the enemies said, Jewish defiance, that is, the Jewish Law. The monks alone did not save the sciences from the surging flood of the migrations of the peoples; the Arabs did valiant work, and the Jews ably assisted them. Without the Arabs and the Jews many sciences might possibly have been submerged during the dark centuries from the death of Jesus to the year 900. Especially astronomy and geometry, medicine, theology, and philosophy were treated and expounded by the Arabs and the Jews of those times, and works on these subjects were translated from the Syriac and the Greek into Arabic and Hebrew, and so made accessible to the scholars of the Occidental world.

Science among the Jews

The important rôle played by the Jews in the advancement of civilization in the above epoch has not yet been sufficiently appreciated. An old legend naïvely says, that the art of healing with all its prescriptions and regulations was taught by God Himself to Adam in Paradise, and that Father Noah carried it with him into the ark. However, what the greatest historian of medicine says, that the "science of medicine cannot be imagined without the participation of the Jews," is an historic truth. The achievements of the Jews cut a figure upon every page of the history of medical science. Jews were the teachers of medicine at the first universities of Europe, Montpellier and Salerno. As early as the ninth century Isaac Israeli wrote a treatise on fever. When the physicians of a later day consulted the book, they saw to their amazement, that modern medicine knows no diagnosis for fever other than that recorded by the physician of a thousand years ago, living on the edge of the wilderness. A Jew was the first to study the refraction of light; a Jew introduced to Europe the famous work of Dioscorides, the foundation of the whole science of botany; a Jew wrote the first textbook of geometry in Europe, and other intellectual feats performed by Jews will come to light when we reach the description of our next period.

Meantime the Jews had found a new home, which received them hospitably, and for some time to come permitted them to pursue their vocations peaceably and devote themselves to intellectual work. The description of this happy era will be the subject of our next paper. Before we pass on to it, we must give a paragraph to a curious phenomenon stirring to its depths the Judaism of the time we are studying. As often before, a man arose among the Jews animated by the desire to exert a reforming influence upon Judaism, if the expression is permissible. His name was Anan. He held the opinion, that much in the Talmud and in the religious laws of Judaism had gotten too far away from the simple, direct meaning of the biblical injunctions. "Read the Scriptures"—this was the watchword that attracted followers in greater and greater numbers as the feeling spread, that the burden of the Law was, indeed, too heavy. They separated from the body of the Jews, and called themselves Karaites. In the beginning it looked as though the new sect would be a menace to Judaism. It throve sturdily, and the energetic rebuff of its assaults by the great men of Israel is evidence

The Karaites

that they were considered a peril. From the ninth to the twelfth century, the sect must have possessed real importance. But instead of delivering Judaism from a yoke, the avowed aim of the Karaites, they would have imposed a new one. If they had been successful, the Jews would now be groaning under the thraldom of Scriptural literalism—additional proof that the Talmud was Judaism's safeguard against spiritual serfdom; additional testimony that in Judaism tradition has never ceased to be a living process. The Karaites rebelled against the Talmud, and became slaves to the letter of the Scriptures. They nowhere attained to a position of importance. At present several hundreds are to be found in the Crimea and in southern Russia. Tshufut Kale, a rock city, is their centre; they possess a very old cemetery there. The Russian government has emancipated them, while the other Jews under its sway are languishing in abject misery. In the spiritual life of the Jews they have only a very small place; they did no injury to Judaism, but they certainly did not promote its welfare.

Long before the Karaites, Jews lived in Russia; in fact, a great Jewish kingdom once existed there. One day the king of the Chazars, for some reason or other, became a convert to the Jewish faith, and with the king, Bulan by name, his whole people accepted Judaism. In Spain, where the Jews were leading happy lives, the rumor of a Jewish kingdom in the north spread far and wide. As the hope in the

Jewish Chazar Kingdom

coming of the Messiah had never been abandoned, the Spanish Jews were quick to yield up their minds to romantic speculations: Perhaps the king of that far-off, unknown land is the Messiah; perhaps he will lead us back to the Holy Land! One of their elect wrote to the king of the Chazars, and his letter has come down to us, a mine of information upon a variety of subjects.

History plays curious tricks with men and things; it follows no fixed laws, and germs sprout spontaneously here and there, only to disappear as suddenly as they came into sight. A legend narrates, that Wladimir Monomachos, Grand Duke of Kiew, one day conceived the idea of setting aside the old gods. He summoned a Christian theologian, a heathen priest, and a Jewish rabbi to carry on a disputation before him, so that he might decide which religion he and his people were to confess. The representative of Christianity won the day, else the Russians were—Jews!

The history of this period, like that of the foregoing ones, ends with a remarkable occurrence. The Academy at Sora, in Babylonia, was in the habit of sending scholars annually to the lands of the diaspora to collect funds from wealthy Jews for the maintenance of the venerable seat of learning. Towards the end of the tenth century, four men were sent on this mission. The vessel on which the scholars embarked was wrecked. Three were saved, and sold as slaves. One drifted to Cairo, one to Kairwan, and the third to Spain. The second became the founder of the study of the Talmud in Northern Africa, and the last carried to Spain the spiritual treasures inherited from centuries of constant intellectual activity, and stimulated his Spanish brethren to devote themselves to their care and to increase them. For, in Spain Israel had found a new home, in which the Jews achieved the best they have ever contributed to the sum of human civilization.

IV

Out of our cold, snowy North, I wish my readers to transport themselves to Spain, the sunny land of wine and song. Of all the countries of the European continent, none exercises such charm upon the student of mediæval history. With Jewish life it seems to have been connected since ancient days by gossamer threads of sympathy, until the bond was snapped asunder by religious fanaticism. As far back as biblical times, the Israelites had intercourse with Spain; witness the prophet Jonah who embarked for Tartessus (Tarshish), a little town of Spain. They had commercial dealings with the extreme western European country, and later, after the destruction of Jerusalem, no doubt can be entertained, that many Jews journeyed thither. With the Romans surely a large number went to Spain, and with equal certainty we may speak of Jewish settlements under the Visigoths. During the first four centuries, the Jews lived in Spain unmolested. So long as the Visigoths professed the Arian doctrine, they served as soldiers, and were employed in state offices. This pleasant aspect of affairs changed with the adoption of the Catholic faith by the ruling race. The oppression of the Jews began, and a full measure of persecution, pain, and misfortune was poured out upon them. No more was this a permanent condition. On a sunny July day of the

Jews in Visigothic Spain

year 711, the situation changed in a trice. It is well known how like a windstorm the Islam passed not only through the desert, but through all the African lands. Not even a century had elapsed since its rise, when the new religion had subjected northern Africa, and was crossing the narrow strait of Gibraltar, separating Africa from Spain.

In the memorable battle of Xeres de la Frontera the Arabs were victorious, and they put to flight the Visigoths. Some say, that the Jews were conspicuous in the battle for intrepid deeds; others say, that they acted as the spies of the Arabs, and were repaid for their services by Arab favor. In either case, a new, happy, prosperous period dawned for Spain with the advent of conquering Islam.

Arabs and Jews working in harmony with each other created the most beautiful, the most magnificent civilization produced by the middle ages, and the time glorified by their achievements is a favorite subject of poet and artist. If the voices of men were silent, thousands of stones would speak, and testify unto the loveliness of the dwelling together of the two races. Under their stimulation, art, poesy, and science began to blossom. At the end of about two centuries, Abdur-Rahmân III was ruler of the whole of Spain; the crescent was planted in all the large cities, in Lucena and in Toledo, in Seville and in Granada. This monarch had a Jewish Grand Vizier, a minister named Chasdaï ibn Shaprut, the previously mentioned writer of the famous letter still extant addressed to the king of the Chazars,

Jews in Moorish Spain

and inquiring of him about the great Jewish realm in the north, the report of which had reached Spain. He was the Caliph's favorite, and wonderful tales are told of his statesmanship, his scientific attainments, his love for Judaism. Twice his skill as a diplomat was successfully put to the test. The first time he was at the head of a deputation from the Caliph to the Byzantine Emperor, and his statecraft compassed the desired end. He did not rest content with the political victory, for he took with him to Europe a book which the world of scholars would have missed sorely, had it not been accessible to them. It was the work on plants by Dioscorides, on which the whole science of botany during the middle ages built itself up. Again he won a diplomatic victory. The Caliph wanted to send him with a deputation, this time to the German Emperor Otto I. It is not known why Chasdaï did not accompany the embassy; none the less his art established peace and an alliance between the German Emperor and the Caliph on terms that earned for him the commendation of both rulers. Yet this man, occupying so exalted a place, was a loyal, pious Jew; what is more, a Jew who supported and advanced the efforts made in all departments of Jewish activity in his day, and nursed into life the germs of the science of Judaism.

The Islam-confessing Arabs were a lucky people in the matter of science and art. They had no hindering, compelling past. Undisturbed by tradition, they could pursue their aims with single-hearted devotion. Greek they probably did not know, and of Hebrew they must have been similarly ignorant, but they believed in an invisible God, Creator of heaven and earth. This was the teaching Mohammed had accepted from Judaism. For the rest, they harbored no prejudice against the adherents of other faiths. Their object was to oppose heathenism, but towards Judaism and Christianity they felt no animosity. It was, therefore, fortunate that they came into mental contact with the Jews in the cloudless Spanish period. The Jews understood Greek, and in conjunction with the Arabs, they translated the scientific literature of the Greeks and Syrians into Arabic, and later, without the collaboration of the Arabs, into Latin. The whole extent of the activity of the Jews as translators was revealed only a few years ago through the devoted industry of a single inquirer, the astonishing result of whose scholarship would seem to have required the strength and duration of ten lives. The Jewish translators were a corps of about two hundred men, physicians, mathematicians, astronomers, philosophers, poets. Their one aim was the translation into Arabic of the most prominent works on philosophy, on the exact sciences, and on the fine arts. In this work the intimacy between Arabs and Jews was so close that to this day it costs minute research to discover whether the translator of a given work was an Arab or a Jew. Very often the race of the author was not mentioned, unless he did it himself. The most celebrated works of poetry preserved in the treasure houses

Jews as Translators

of India, Persia, and Arabia, became known to European students only by the mediation of the Jews. The modern scholar is right who maintains that the root and source of all our romances, novels, fables, fairy lore, and ballads, are to be sought in the few books, six or eight perhaps, that the Arabs and the Jews rescued from oblivion by transplanting them to Europe from out of the gorgeous splendor of the Orient, the flower-strewn meadows of India and Persia.

Their scientific work is of still higher importance. The greatest thinker of the ancient Greek world, it is universally conceded, was Aristotle. His philosophy was destined to dominate the middle ages; he became the sole ruler in the realm of the science of sciences, and the Jews should always account it a distinction that they contributed to the establishment of his power. It is unlikely that the Arabs would have been able to familiarize themselves with his philosophy, if it had not reached them through the medium of the Jewish mind. Strictly construed, Arabic philosophy was atheistic, and Aristotle's system, a reconciliation of reason with religion, could not have obtained currency, had Jewish teachers not assumed the task of harmonizing them. The Jews translated Aristotle's works and those of other Greek thinkers into Arabic. Two hundred years later, when the exigencies of the times required the change of idiom, they put them into Latin. Curiously enough, after the golden glory of the Spanish period had paled, and the grave-like gloom of ignorance and mysticism had spread its pall even over the Jewish camp, Jewish scholars again arose who translated the same works from Latin into Hebrew—a remarkable play of events and circumstances, of absorbing interest to the historian of civilization. Similarly, in the field of mathematics, in that of astronomy, of medicine, in short, in all the sciences known and cultivated at the time, their achievements were distinguished and important; in part they even did pioneer work.

For us the most noteworthy feature is that the men participating in this work were pious Jews. In the Spain of that day, the Jews enjoyed equal rights and privileges with the other citizens. They participated in jousts and tournaments, served in the army, occupied a respected position at court, and in the song contests in the Alhambra Jewish poets were among the competitors. Yet they remained Jews in spirit, in feeling, in faith, in conviction.

Not only in the secular arts and sciences is Jewish endeavor to be credited with brilliant results; also in the sphere of Jewish intellectual activity it reached heights not scaled since, and probably never again to be scaled. Hebrew poetry put forth blossom after blossom, and as once on the banks of the Jordan, the harp of Zion gave forth sweet, soothing melody. *Neo-Hebrew Poetry* The three greatest poets were Solomon Gabirol, Moses ben Ezra, and Jehuda Halevi. Gabirol stands at the beginning of the period of prolific production, which closes with Jehuda Halevi, the prince of all its poets, in whom the brilliant rays illuminating it converge. He was a popular physician in Saragossa and a distinguished philosopher besides. The philosophic work that he has left us treats soberly and sensibly of the agreement between faith and reason. Beloved though he was in his city and community, he determined, after he had passed his fiftieth year, to leave Spain. He gave up his circle of disciples, his family, his admirers, in order to end his life in Palestine, the land he loved, the object of his intensest longing. A number of poems composed on the journey have been handed down to us; one of the most beautiful is the description of a storm at sea. In other scattered poems, he tells of his arrival upon the soil of the Holy Land. Suddenly his harp falls silent, and we know nothing of the fortunes of his last days, nor where he died. Busily-weaving legend, however, more merciful than history, has surrounded his death with the halo of poetry. It tells us—and if it is not true, it a least accords well with his character—that arrived at the gates of the Holy City, he sang, as he stood absorbed in the contemplation of the scene before him, his glorious Zion song, repeated to this day, on the Ninth of Ab, in the synagogues of all the lands on earth. While he was apostrophizing the city of his dreams and yearnings, a Saracen rider galloped over him, and under the hoofs of the horse he breathed forth his soul. A modern poet, Heinrich Heine, has introduced him into Occidental literature:

[marginal note: Jehuda Halevi]

"Ay, he was a master singer,
Brilliant pole-star of his age.
Light and beacon to his people!
Wondrous mighty was his singing—

Verily a fiery pillar,
Moving on 'fore Israel's legions,
Restless caravan of sorrow,
Through the exile's desert plain."

Jehuda Halevi closed the succession of the great poets of neo-Hebrew literature, but poetic inspiration did not die out altogether. In accordance with the laws of human development and decline, the epoch of great spiritual expansion was followed by one of lesser resplendence. Form and color were poured out upon it lavishly; the great themes reappeared, but the master minds had vanished never to return. In the field of philosophy the same phenomenon took place. Here Moses Maimonides was the last of the original inquirers. His life and intellectual activity set the seal of their inspiration upon the scientific endeavor that followed. Moreover, they kindled a stubborn conflict, which had the effect of clarifying the convictions of thinkers as well as of the nation at large. I should have to write many a page, were I to mention only the most prominent and important of the men whose names are connected with blessed attainment.

Moses Maimonides

The alliance between Jews and Arabs produced on the whole a harmonious public life. In spite of some dark spots—for collisions occurred between them, nor need it be told that the Jews bore the costs—the picture is flooded with sunshine, as long as the Arabs were the masters of Spain. Chasdaï ibn Shaprut was not the only Jew holding the office of minister to a caliph. Samuel the Prince, for instance, occupied the same position. He was a dealer in spices at Malaga. Being the only great calligrapher in the city, everybody, not excepting the minister, resorted to him when a letter was to be written. Some of these letters fell into the hands of the Caliph Habus, who marvelled not only at their beautiful execution, but also at the profundity and charm of their contents. He sent for the spice merchant, and found him to be a man of extraordinary sagacity and experience. The Caliph had him come and live in his palace, and Samuel rose higher and higher, until he reached the position of counsellor to the Caliph. His dazzling fortune did not banish his brethren in faith from his mind; he remained a loyal Jew. We have some of his neo-Hebrew poems, and we know him to have been an intelligent promoter of all endeavors calculated to elevate Judaism.

<small>Samuel the Prince</small>

It is impossible to say what course Jewish development would have taken, had the Jews been vouchsafed the good fortune of pursuing their aims in social, political, and intellectual life peaceably and quietly in co-operation with the Arabs. For a time it had seemed that the old curse pronounced in Leviticus, that "the sound of a leaf shaken shall chase them," had been removed from the Jews; almost it had

<small>Jews in Christian Spain</small>

seemed that they were, not accursed, but blessed. In a little while, however, political affairs assumed an ominous aspect. Masters though the Arabs were of Spain, they were not able to eradicate the national spirit surviving from former centuries. Even when Abdur-Rahmân III ruled the whole peninsula, the old Christian-Roman attitude of mind prevailed, particularly in northern Spain. A constant struggle went on between Arabic, Jewish, and Christian-Roman culture. But the example of tolerance set by the Arab caliphs did not fail to work its effect upon the Christian kings, who, step by step, recovered Spanish territory from the Arabs. Even under Christian dominion, the Jews were tolerated, respected, and to some extent favored. By certain incidents we can judge of the happy conditions that prevailed. Alfonso X, for instance, sent for Isaac ibn Sid, the precentor of a synagogue, and charged him with the computation of the astronomical tables to this day bearing the king's name, the "Alfonsine Tables." This is but one manifestation of the cordial relations existing between the adherents of the two religions. We might multiply indefinitely the number of prominent men who remained Jews despite high preferment. The Arab example, moreover, took effect outside of Spain. Frederick II, the German emperor, sent to Spain for Jewish scholars in order to have them translate celebrated works on art from Greek into Latin, and Robert of Anjou and many other princes followed suit. This relation, too, was doomed to undergo change. The larger the territory gained by Christianity in Spain, the further the sign of the crescent had to retreat, the more harassed became the condition of the Spanish Jews.

We have not the details of the intercourse of the Jews of Spain with those of northern France and Germany. Nor do we know what measures, if any, they took to avert the troublous fate of their less fortunate brethren. The three centuries from the ninth to the twelfth may be considered the period during which the Catholic Church arrived at the determination to extirpate every vestige of Judaism. Naturally, the condition of the Jews in the lands under the sway of Rome was abjectly gloomy. What the German Jews suffered during the crusades is matter of general knowledge; from Breslau to Mayence the road was marked with the blood and strewn with the bodies of our ancestors, fathers and mothers, the old and the young. No more heartrending tragedy than the persecutions that the Jews of Germany had to undergo in those days has ever been enacted in history. They afford us examples, not only of exalted capacity for suffering, but of unparalleled heroism. We hear of a father murdering his own children to save them from forcible baptism; of a mother casting her daughters into the Rhine rather than expose them to the persecution of approaching troops; of an aged man throwing a firebrand into a synagogue to preserve it from imminent desecration by crusaders. In short, the marvels of the martyrdom of the German Jews are as little to be exhausted as those of the glory of

The Crusades

their Spanish brethren. In 1290 the Jews were banished from England, in 1305 from France by Philip the Fair, and that they were not driven out of Germany was due to the minute territorial division of the Empire among numerous rulers. In one place they were tolerated because their money could not be spared; in another a prince reigned who needed them as agents of various kinds; and in a third place the ruler bore with them as the *servi cameræ* of the Holy Roman Empire.

<small>Persecutions of the Jews</small>

Pope Innocent III more than any one man is to be held responsible for the unchaining of the storms of religious fanaticism against the Jews. He enforced the decrees confining them to special Jews' quarters, and compelling them to wear long black cloaks, three-cornered hats, and yellow badges upon their garments, so as to ensure their being recognized everywhere as Jews and being treated with due contempt. Islam was able to accept the existence of Judaism with toleration, for it had not begun its course with a bias to which it had to conform, regardless of consequences. With Christianity the case was different. From the first it had proclaimed itself the fulfilment of Judaism. If Christianity had indeed superseded Judaism, the latter could not be permitted to continue. No Jew could be allowed to exist, for his presence bore testimony against Christianity. The lowliest, the most despised Jew was a living protest against the doctrines of the new religion. Only from this point of view we may judge of the zeal for persecution under which Judaism suffered for centuries at the hands of popes and emperors, princes and bishops, no less than of nations. A dark picture, and it makes it only too plain how it came about that a people, mercilessly oppressed, and chased like a dry leaf from spot to spot all over the globe, became narrow in mind and "short of spirit." The Jews retired more and more within themselves; ever smaller grew the part they took in the joys and sorrows of the nations in whose midst they lived, and gradually they confined themselves altogether to the contracted circle of Talmud studies.

By the beginning of the fourteenth century, the situation in Spain had developed to the point at which the Arabs were retreating fast with no hope of retrieving their fortune, and the Christian kings were enjoying an uninterrupted succession of victories. It is not possible here to describe in detail the development of affairs in a country divided up among many rulers, as Spain was. Suffice it to say that had the Spaniards known gratitude, they would have been forced to acknowledge the services of the Jews. Despite the lowering horizon, however, the Jews were still taking part in the intellectual life of Spain. One king tolerated and favored them; another persecuted and banished them.

The literature of Spain, as might be expected, is thoroughly Catholic. Of all literatures it is the most religious. If the expression is permissible, I should say, that it nestles in the heart of the

Catholic Church. It is filled with the most unquestioning reverence for the dogmas of Catholicism. How curious, then, that Jews should have sat at the cradle of Spanish literature. When the Spanish speak of their greatest epic, they mean the *Cid*, well known to students of German literature through Herder's translation: the *Cid* is based upon the chronicles of a Jew, Ibn Faradsh. A Jew wrote the first Spanish romance; a Jew wrote the first Spanish drama, *Celestina;* a Jew was the first Spanish troubadour, and the last Spanish troubadour, the tailor (*il ropero*), was also a Jew, who lived at a time when forced baptisms were the order of the day for Jews. {Jews in Spanish Literature}

Romance literature experienced a revival a little later, and it is significant that the most important poet of the period again was a Jew, a Brazilian by birth, Antonio José de Silva, whose life offers a signal illustration of the reward Israel has always reaped from the nations of the earth for his spiritual achievements. {Antonio José de Silva} This Antonio lived at the beginning of the eighteenth century, and was the most distinguished poet in the parent land of Portugal where he had settled. He was called the second Calderon, for he composed some seventy plays, which were performed at Lisbon before the court. When he appeared in the street, the people shouted, "Our Antonio!" His cleverness and his wit endeared him to all, and he was one of the most celebrated men in Portugal. One day the rumor spread, that Antonio was a secret Jew; that, in fact, he and his brethren in faith met in the cellar of his house for divine worship according to the Jewish rite. The information reached the Inquisition, which spared neither person nor rank. He had to appear before the dread tribunal, and was questioned on the truth of the rumor. Was he too proud to deny it, or did he place too much confidence in the saving power of his popularity? Be that as it may, he was incarcerated, and condemned to suffer death. One day the aristocratic world of Lisbon attended a "first performance:" in the open square before the cathedral the greatest poet of the land was burnt at the stake. Out of the flames, the noble lords and ladies heard strange, unintelligible words. Antonio was meeting death in good Jewish hero and martyr fashion, upon his lips the confession of faith: "Hear, O Israel, the Lord our God is one!" So died the last great dramatist of Romance literature, "the Portuguese Plautus."

We have anticipated the course of events, but the end of the great drama of Jewish history in Spain is well known. The more widespread the influence acquired by the Christian kings, the more hopeless became the position of the Jews. In the fourteenth century we begin to hear of forced conversions and new-Christians, that is, such as adopted Christianity for one or the other reason. The numbers reported may be exaggerated; Jewish chroniclers estimate them at hundreds of thousands. On one

The Marranos

day, in some city or other, from twenty to thirty thousand were forced to submit to baptism; their conviction was not consulted. Naturally these forced converts did not immediately give up all intercourse with their former coreligionists, nor need we be surprised to learn, that many secretly held fast to their old faith. The new-Christians were the most distinguished victims of the cruelty of the Inquisition. Finally the day came, when the last and most relentless blow was to be dealt the hated Jews. Innocent III in his time had realized, that if Christianity was ever to obtain complete sway over Spain, warfare would have to be waged against the Jews, who from the first had enjoyed respect and power, and had displayed intellectual strength. The pope's plan was destined to succeed in the reign of their Catholic majesties, Ferdinand and Isabella. With a strong arm, Ferdinand had begun the last assault upon the Arabs, who had entrenched themselves for the final struggle in Granada, their remaining stronghold. In 1492 they were dispossessed, and with a last sigh, *il ultimo sospiro di moro*, Boabdil, the last Moorish king, attended by a few faithful followers —the subject of a familiar picture—turned his face to the Alpujarras, and from the mosque of Granada floated the sign of the cross over the whole of Spain.

Now came the turn of the Jews. The country had been cleared of Arabs, the Jews were to share their fate. The Grand Inquisitor Torquemada has won the dubious fame of having achieved Jewish ruin. He was successful in persuading the king, still more successful in persuading the queen, that oppression and persecution were inadequate measures, and that Spain would be a Christian country only after the last Jew had been banished from its soil. In the same year, 1492, Ferdinand signed the calamitous edict by the terms of which all Jews were exiled from Spain. The Jews of that time still enjoyed respect; intellectually they held a position of influence, and many wealthy people, farmers of the public revenues and high city officials, were among them. These prominent members of the race did all in their power to prevent the promulgation of the edict. The negotiations culminated in a highly dramatic scene, which has often been the theme of painters. A Jewish deputation, at whose head is a famous Jewish scholar, stands before the royal couple in the palace, and offers them thirty thousand ducats to rescind the cruel decree. A door opens suddenly, and Torquemada appears on the threshold, bearing a huge cross in his arms. "Judas Iscariot," he exclaimed, "sold his Master for thirty pieces of silver, and your Majesties are about to sell him for thirty thousand." The fate of the Jews was sealed; Ferdinand and Isabella dismissed the deputation.

On the Ninth of Ab, the ominous day on which the Jews had so often suffered woe and misery, three hundred thousand Jews left Spain, the beautiful land in which they had lived unmolested for more than five hundred years, and which they had enriched with a succession of distinguished thinkers, poets, and statesmen, as well as with its first and its last troubadour. Their possessions, with the exception of their gold and silver, they were permitted to carry with them. Precipitately they had to dispose of their real estate, and then they left with what they could save from the wreck. The rabbis, it is reported, ordered cymbals and trumpets to be sounded at the head of the column of exiles from each town, to drown the cries, and sobs, and groans of the many thousands that had to leave their home and knew not whither to turn.

The banishment of the Jews from Spain is the closing scene of a tragedy. By a remarkable train of circumstances, by the irony of history, one is tempted to say, it happened that on the very day on which the Jews were compelled to leave Spain, a Christian, Christopher Columbus, left the Spanish land to discover a new world. His expedition was equipped with the money confiscated from the exiled Jews; the physician accompanying the little fleet was a Jew; a Jewish sailor is said to have been the first to sight land; a Jew was the first to establish a settlement on the hospitable shores of America.

The workings of a divine Providence can be traced at every step in the history of the world and in the history of Judaism—this is the sublime, uplifting lesson that forces itself upon the consideration of all who open the annals of history, and follow up the sufferings, the wanderings, and the sorrows of our people from century to century.

V

THE banishment of the Jews from Spain, the grand *finale* of the fourth period of Jewish history, was an event of decisive importance for the whole of Jewry. In no land had the position of the Jews been so remarkable as in Spain. There it had presented the rare union of civil and social eminence with loyalty and self-forgetful devotion to Judaism. The Jewish mind had not experienced a similar period of efflorescence since the days of the Babylonian Academies, or since the fullest expansion of national life in Palestine, and I fear that there is no hope of another like it. It is, therefore, natural that the blow that felled to the ground the Jews of Spain should have reacted upon Judaism as a whole.

The Spanish Exiles The three hundred thousand Jews who had to leave Spain on the Ninth of Ab, 1492, were scattered through all the European countries, and of necessity introduced new currents of thought into the spiritual life of their brethren long settled there. As for their material treasures, they, too, were scattered, and soon had disappeared. As I said before, they were permitted to carry away with them only a small part of their possessions; still, the fortunes they rescued from confiscation are estimated at high figures. However great they might have been, their needs absorbed all in a short time. Only a few reached the countries offering them a refuge as wealthy men. But possessions of other kinds the Jews brought: first, their unusual experiences; second, an abundant store of scientific knowledge, which they had won in Spain, and in the promotion of which they had done valiant service; and third, the valuable social culture they had acquired.

There remained in Spain a considerable portion of the people, those mentioned before who either defiantly or willingly had submitted to the order of things, and had accepted Christianity. They were called pseudo-Christians, or Marranos. Their number has probably been exaggerated by historians, Jewish and Christian, who estimate it at hundreds of thousands. It happened, to be sure, that in one city, on one day, ten, fifteen, and, on one occasion, possibly twenty thousand Jews were forced to accept Christianity; but these figures should be used with caution. The condition of the Spanish Marranos was much sadder than that of the Jews before their banishment. That they had yielded to baptism under compulsion was not forgotten; they were not credited with sincerity, and in the eyes of the world remained Jews to the end of the chapter. Still the Marranos succeeded in working their way into prominent places, as was only natural. Spain had deprived herself of so large a number of useful citizens, that the loss had to be made good in some fairly acceptable way, if the state machinery was to continue in smooth operation. The Marranos moved into the places vacated by the exiled Jews, and at the end of a century the highest offices were filled by them. They were the ministers and the professors, and the whole of the Spanish nobility, to use the expression of a Spanish poet, was "Judaized," inoculated with Jewish blood. In fact, some of the most zealous agents of the Inquisition were apostate Jews; even the names of Jewish Inquisitors and Grand Inquisitors are recorded in the annals of Jewish history. The importance of the Marranos in public life is aptly characterized by a cleverly invented anecdote, ascribed to the Marquis de Pombal, minister to the king of Portugal, who had imitated his cousin of Spain in banishing the Jews from his realm. One day, the king of Portugal, whose counsellors had probably reported to him that the neo-Christians were usurping the choice places in the state, and were working harm to the public weal, published a rescript ordering all Marranos to wear a yellow hat as a badge. The next day, his minister Pombal appeared before him with three yellow hats, and when the king asked him, for whom the first was intended, he answered: "For myself, your Majesty." "And for whom is the second?" asked the king. "For your Majesty's Grand Inquisitor." "And who is to wear the third hat?" "Your Majesty." To so great an extent was the blood of Spain and Portugal mixed with Jewish blood.

The countries in which the Jewish exiles settled at once were Brazil, North Africa, Italy, Holland, Turkey, and Poland. The consequences for Spain were such as a study of political economy and history might lead one to expect. From the day it rid itself of its Jews, the land whose king had once been monarch of the civilized world began to sink, until it fell to the position of a power of the second or third rank through the indolence and impotence of its rulers. To this day it has not recovered from the self-inflicted blow. The lands offering an asylum to the Jews derived corresponding benefit from their presence, showing itself partly at once, partly in the course of time, and calculable by years and in coin.

While the fate of the Spanish Jews was working itself out, a new time was dawning. Among all the movements that have stirred and advanced the spiritual life of humanity, two in particular rouse our lively interest and absorb our attention whenever we open the book of history. The Renaissance in Italy and Humanism in Germany close the middle ages, and conjure up the new time. *The Renaissance and Humanism* The Renaissance first broke the power of the Church in Italy, loosing the fetters of servitude and fanaticism from the minds of men, raising them to the height of human dignity, and proclaiming liberty of knowledge for all the sons of earth. A series of stimulating events, material and spiritual, form the introduction to the new era: The discovery of America enlarged the horizon of men; inventions and discoveries opened a vista of unnumbered possibilities; gunpowder destroyed the feudal castles of the knights of chivalry; the art of printing lent wings to human thought; the Copernican system taught a new view of nature; and finally came the Reformation, purging and elevating religious thought. It is our boast, that Jews had a share in all the new activities. In general, no intellectual movement of importance has been urged down to the present day, in which Jews have failed to take the part of pioneers and promoters.

When the Renaissance exhumed the world of classic antiquity, bringing to the light of day the treasures of Hellas buried under the mould of monasteries, the Bible incidentally stepped into its rightful inheritance, and when Humanism cleansed Christianity of the dross attaching to it, Jewish antiquity again succeeded to the enjoyment of its due. The leaders of the Italian Renaissance were the disciples of Jewish teachers, and the Humanists threaded their way through antiquity at the hands of Jewish rabbis and instructors. In his youth Martin Luther had seen the Bible chained in the monastery at Erfurt. The reading of the book was deemed a crime in the Catholic Church; only the prelates and the high dignitaries were permitted to use it. Martin Luther struck off the chain, and restored the Bible to the German people —a spiritual achievement of immortal worth, surpassing all else he did. But it should not be forgotten, that Martin Luther followed in the footsteps of an erudite Rabbi, whom the older generation of Jews remember from school studies and from his authoritative influence upon their religious thought. Rashi (Solomon ben Isaac) was his name, one of the most prominent of the Bible commentators of the middle ages, who won distinguished fame by the simplicity, directness, and clearness of his method of explaining the Bible. Two hundred years after his death his work was used by a Franciscan monk, Nicholas de Lyra, whose annotations of the Bible for Christian communities became the basis for Luther's Bible translation. It is not going too far, then, to say, that without Rashi Luther can scarcely be imagined—another proof of the interaction of spiritual agencies among different nations, which fanaticism, superstition, and mistrust have not been able to interrupt or trammel. Martin Luther was friendly towards the Jews in the days of his youth. He advocated their cause warmly, and cautioned the German nobility against persecuting and oppressing them. In later life, after he had passed through the saddening experiences growing out of his great work of the Reformation, never more than half finished, his feelings underwent a change, and in his declining years he became a bitter opponent of the Jews.

Very different in this respect was the course of another promulgator of the new faith, the early champion of the ideas applied by Luther, John Reuchlin, "Germania's phœnix," as he was proudly called, one of the noblest and most liberal minds of the German nation. Early in life he had devoted himself, like the heroes of the Italian Renaissance, to the study of Jewish antiquity, and like them had interested himself with peculiar sympathy in one Jewish movement in particular. During the last centuries of the Spanish-Jewish era, when the freedom of the intellectual life was hampered, the prodigious development to which philosophy had attained among the Jews was arrested by an antagonistic force, which, to the hurt of Judaism, made itself supreme, and remained dominant in the following centuries. The new power was the Kabbala. Dropping weary and fatigued from the regions of abstract thought to which it had soared, the Jewish mind was floundering in the mazy depths of mysticism. It pondered on the problems of human life and of the world of phenomena in a way far removed from the rational speculations of true philosophy. The movement had not sprung up over night. In general, spiritual agencies are slow in gathering force, though usually they assert their fully developed strength unexpectedly and in places remote from those in which their first germs were planted. So the mystic movement seems to have leaped to maturity at a bound; suddenly Jewish life was overgrown by it, and all other spiritual endeavor pushed into the background. The historian has nothing more to do than state the existence of the movement; the psychologist must be appealed to, if we are curious to know, why Christians as well as Jews were drawn to the mystic view of life. The enlightened leaders of the Renaissance and the Humanist chiefs in Germany alike studied Kabbalistic works. Reuchlin was no exception, and his enthusiastic admiration for Judaism grew, the better he became acquainted with the Jews and the spiritual treasures amassed by them in every department.

The Kabbala

Even while Reuchlin's importance was gaining widespread recognition, a movement arose among the opponents of Humanism aiming at the humiliation of the Humanists and thereby at the downfall of the Jews. A Dominican, Jacob von Hoogstraten, was the promoter of the movement, and his mentor is said to have been an apostate from Judaism, Pfefferkorn by name, one of the first of the succession of apostate Jews who brought woe and misery upon their former coreligionists. The matter came before the Diet and Emperor Maximilian I. Heavy artillery was brought into requisition by the Dominicans. They tried to prove that certain malevolent rules of conduct appeared in the sacred books of the Jews; they asserted that in the course of one of their prayers the Jews spit out in scorn of the other nations, and deliver them over to shame and death, and that at the Passover they use the blood of Christian children in the preparation of the unleavened bread. They enumerated the whole long list of aspersions and lies that have since been adduced whenever the ruin of the Jews has been contemplated. Then Reuchlin stepped forth, the man of courage, not intimidated by the reproach "Jew servant," not silenced by the rumor that he had been bought with Jewish money. He brought his whole apparatus of scholarship, acquired through years of labor and application, to bear upon the demonstration of the malice and scurrility of the calumnies. Again the Jews were saved. The decree ordering

The Pfefferkorn Episode

the burning of the Talmud was recalled, and Reuchlin was victorious over the obscurantists. The quarrel dragged its slow length along, until at last, long after Reuchlin's death, as all readers of history know, the Humanists vanquished the enemies of "sweetness and light." The end was that the bold Austin friar ventured to nail his ninety-five theses on the church door of Wittenberg, and so brought about a complete revolution in religious thought.

The material condition of the Jews in the time when they were the teachers of the prominent leaders of the Renaissance and of Humanism, as well as of cardinals and popes, was most woe-begone. The sunlight of the new time was glorifying the world, but to the Jew each day brought a renewal of oppression and persecution, so that the "tribes of the wandering foot" never dared lay aside their staff.

When they were seeking new sojourning places, the countries named above, especially Turkey, Holland, and Poland, were the first to offer them permanent refuges. Sultan Bajazed, on being told that Ferdinand had banished the Jews from the Spanish lands, is said to have exclaimed: "And you call this king wise, who has deprived himself of his best subjects?" He did not fail to execute the policy suggested as the correct one in his rebuke, for Turkey was opened wide for the reception of the Jews. There they have never had to suffer severe oppression. Within a few decades of their settlement in Turkey, we

The Jews in Turkey

hear of the Sultan's Jewish physician-in-ordinary, Moses Hamon, an energetic and sagacious promoter of spiritual endeavors. Among the first works issuing from the printing press—this, too, is characteristic of the intellectual constitution of the Jews—were Jewish books, one of them a Hebrew Bible published by Jews. The first Hebrew printing presses were set up in Italy and Turkey.

Less than a century after the Jews had settled peaceably in Turkey, they produced a succession of distinguished men who enjoyed the dignities and the respect the Jews in Spain had possessed. One of them was a forcibly baptized Jew, a Marrano, who had escaped from Portugal in his youth. *Don Joseph Nassi* With the remnants of his fortune Don Joseph Nassi founded a banking house in Antwerp, and when fortune refused to smile on him, he went to Turkey, where he rose to high estate. At the same time, his aunt, Donna Gracia Mendesia, came by way of Venice and other places from Portugal to Turkey. Her daughter Reyna was celebrated for wit and beauty, and it was natural that she and Don Joseph should become a pair. Such honors were showered upon them that, were it not attested by history beyond a doubt, their good fortune would be deemed impossible in days the saddest of the middle ages for the Jews, when hundreds of them were daily being led to the slaughter in Germany, and hundreds were languishing under the tortures of the Inquisition in Spain. In such times Sultan Selim II made the Jew Joseph Nassi duke of Naxos in return for his diplomatic services, and it seems certain that he was prevented by death alone from making him king of Cyprus, as he had intended. Joseph's influence as a diplomat was so powerful, that on one occasion he restored peace among the most important of the European powers, and though the French government objected to the intervention of a Jew in the affairs of the Christian nations, and intrigued against him at the Porte, the Sultan upheld and strengthened him in his position. In spite of the honored place occupied by him in the world of European politics, Don Joseph Nassi never swerved from his faith. He supported every Jewish endeavor, and promoted the science of Judaism. We have coins struck in his honor and in the honor of his mother-in-law, both of whom are given most extravagant praise for their patronage of all things Jewish.

At the time when Joseph Nassi was at the height of his glory, a little Jew lived in Constantinople, the physician Solomon Ashkenasi, who later rose to almost as exalted a place as Nassi's. The Sultan appointed him the diplomatic representative of Turkey at Venice, then mistress on land and sea, the most puissant of European governments. Despite intrigues and opposition, he maintained himself at his post for over twenty years. The Jews of Venice were confined (1516) in a Jews' quarter, the Ghetto; under the potent influence of the Jesuits, the new order, Italy began to pollute herself with the persecutions until then characteristic only of Spain and

Germany; the papal censor was occupied in mutilating, in some cases in destroying, the recently printed copies of the Talmud; and in the palace next to that of the doges resided—the Jew, Solomon Ashkenasi, as the respected representative of the Porte. When the European powers were passing through one of their periodic paroxysms, this time on account of the succession to the Polish throne, coveted by France for Henry of Anjou, by Austria for the Archduke Maximilian, and by Poland for the Polish Count Potocki, Solomon Ashkenasi's sagacity brought about the election of Henry of Anjou, the candidate most likely to re-establish the prosperity of unhappy Poland. A letter of his has come down to us, addressed to a correspondent in Poland, in which he says: "The Bishop of Acre will probably claim the credit for himself, but you know that it was I who decided the contest about the Polish crown."

In Holland the situation of the Jews was equally favorable. At the end of the sixteenth century a vessel destined for another port accidentally put in at the Emden harbor. *The Jews in Holland* Moses Phœbus, one of the small colony of Jews at Emden, begged the new arrivals not to remain there, but to proceed to Holland, a liberal country and open to the Jews; he was willing to go with them, he said. The men so led to Amsterdam were the founders of the name and fame of its great congregation, of which Moses Phœbus became the first rabbi. He boasted of having received back into Judaism over twenty thousand Marranos, refugees from Spain. Barely fifty years after their arrival in Amsterdam, the Jews occupied the respected position always attained by them, wherever air and sunlight are not denied them.

Among the Marranos was the family Espinosa, whose son Baruch was a pupil at the Talmud Torah school of Amsterdam. The instruction given at the Jewish institution did not satisfy his ambition. He was lured away by the spirit of the new time, which pervaded the Holland of his day. The path he chose was broad and long, leading him further and further away from the ideas and teachings of the old *Beth ha-Midrash*, until he, Benedict Spinoza, originated a new view of life, a new philosophical system. He was not the only person of note produced by the Marranos of Holland: there were poets and thinkers, diplomats, officers, warriors valiant in the service of their country, and distinguished women, who cut a figure in society. One of the most interesting members of the Dutch-Portuguese colony was Manasseh ben Israel, who enjoyed intimate intercourse with the most prominent Dutch scholars, and maintained a correspondence with the queen of Sweden, urging her to grant Jews the freedom of her country. He turned his attention also to England, whence the Jews had been banished since 1290. In a characteristic letter, which we still possess, addressed to Cromwell, he acquaints the Protector of the Commonwealth with the state of the Jews in various countries, and with the advantages sure to accrue to

England, if she received Jews as citizens. He was invited to appear before Parliament to present his case in person. From that day the movement dates ending in the resettlement of the Jews in England, the country in which they have since lived unmolested as respected citizens.

Now as to the third country, Poland. There, too, the state of affairs was most favorable to the Jews. Poland lacked a middle class; its population consisted of nobles and peasants only. By nature the Jews are representatives of the middle class of society, mediators between the nobility and the peasantry. As early as the beginning of the sixteenth century, the Primate of Poland complained that at the schools Jewish pupils were sitting next to Christian children upon the selfsame benches, and that Jewish parents were sending their sons to Padua and Bologna to study medicine. The enlightened monarchs of Poland employed Jewish diplomats in the capacity of chancellors, as their most intimate advisers. In short, the condition of the Jews in Poland was most satisfactory in those days, and without a doubt Judaism would have attained to noble achievement on Polish soil, had not the unfortunate Cossack rebellion under the leadership of Bogdan Chmelnizky proved a catastrophe for the Jews. It is said, that when Chmelnizky had been captain of the Cossacks, he had been deceived by a Jew. According to another report, his hatred of Jews arose from their having been the framers of all the taxes, the payment of which

The Jews in Poland

he probably resisted. At all events, against the Jews his hatred was more virulent even than against the Poles. For three years, from 1648 to 1651, wholesale massacres were enacted, and trustworthy chroniclers report that between Wilna and Lemberg, over a quarter of a million of Jews were butchered amid the most horrible tortures. It was long before the Jews recovered from the wounds inflicted by the Cossack rebellion. Many of them emigrated, and so it happened, that the Jews once expelled from Germany returned thither.

The intellectual development of the Jews in Poland was neither normal nor healthy; the social oppression they suffered quenched the light of science. The Kabbala had taken all minds captive, and persecution, cutting off contact with outer influences, had induced concentration of all powers upon the study of the Talmud. So extraordinary an endowment of intelligence and intellect as that of the Polish Jews, devoted to a single field, necessarily led to mental stagnation and ossification.

We now approach the movement most characteristic of the period of Jewish history under consideration. At the very time when a Baruch Spinoza was setting forth philosophic ideas so profound that their elaboration still gives employment to scholars and thinkers, his brethren in Turkey, in the whole of the Orient in fact, as well as in Germany and Poland, were taken captive, mind and heart, by an adventurer, whose charm lay in nothing more than his

The Sabbatians

address and his beauty. His name was Sabbatai Zevi, and he was born at Smyrna in 1626. It is not known what qualities the man possessed enabling him to deceive the distrustful, cautious, prudent Jews for nearly half a century; but it is certain that he started a movement fraught with dire consequences for Judaism.

In his twentieth year, Sabbatai had cast off his second wife. He lived at a time when the advent of the Messiah was daily looked forward to with yearning. Cunning deceivers took advantage of the strong emotion of the Jews. Some asserted, that the Messiah would come in 1635, and gather the Jews unto Palestine; others predicted redemption for another year. When Sabbatai made his appearance, the people were prepared to hail him as the Messiah come to redeem the Jews. At the head of his followers, he went straight to Jerusalem. On the soil of the Holy Land, his pretensions to the Messiahship would certainly be vindicated or invalidated. He married a third wife, Sarah, who had had a most singular career. During the confusion of the Cossack rebellion, she had been put, as a child of six years of age, into a Polish nunnery, and had been forced to accept baptism. Later she escaped, and the Jews found her one morning in the Jewish cemetery. They took her under their care, and Sarah returned to the faith of her fathers. After various adventures and journeyings, she came by way of Frankfort on the Main and Leghorn to Smyrna. Sabbatai and Sarah were accompanied by an army of deceived deceivers, enthusiasts and impostors, and not a few honest believers in his Messianic mission as redeemer. The procession wended its way through European lands, finally reaching Turkey. So greatly had the number of his train increased by new accessions, even of very pious Jews, that the Grand Vizier of the Porte took fright, and cited Sabbatai before his tribunal. In his cunning way he succeeded in making it plain to the Vizier, that no sort of danger threatened the Porte; that his one object was to gather together the Jews from all the countries of the world and lead them back to Palestine, where a new Jerusalem awaited them. The Sultan, however, refused to give him credence. He was confined in the tower at Abydos, the "Tower of Strength," as it was called by his adherents, who surrounded it for weeks and months. One day they noticed Turkish guards of honor take Sabbatai Zevi from his prison, and escort him to Constantinople. He had discovered a way out of his difficulties. Believing that his game was over, or that he would be enabling himself to play a rôle on another stage, he had accepted Islam. But the popular movement once set afoot could not be restrained. The report spread, that not Sabbatai, only his phantom double, had turned Mohammedan. So he resumed his place at the head of his Jewish followers. Never had he been more recklessly audacious than at the time when he stood revealed a deceiver. The decrees issued by him in those days close with the words: "I, your God, Sabbatai Zevi!" However, he found it impossible to retain the old respected position for any length of time. After his death, which occurred in Turkey, the movement assumed greater proportions than ever before. Almost in every decade a new Sabbatian adventurer arose, the most dangerous of all in Poland.

There a community of Sabbatians existed as late as the middle of the last century, when fresh life was infused into it by the appearance of a new prophet, Jacob Frank, who faithfully imitated the course of his ideal. He, too, put upon his banner the inscription: "Against the Talmud and for Sabbatai Zevi!" This watchword naturally enlisted the lively sympathy of the Catholic clergy of Poland. Frank was deprived of his liberty; he, too, bought freedom by the acceptance of Christianity, and no less than Sabbatai lost all influence by his cowardly apostasy. The adherents of the Sabbatian movement became stubborn in the degree in which they were threatened with dangers by the secular authorities or the other Jews. In Poland they exist in small numbers to this day, under the name Frankists, the last remnants of a disastrous movement that split Judaism into two or three camps, and stunted every ideal endeavor. Even the Jews of Germany, who enjoyed a higher degree of culture than those in Poland and the East, took part in it, and great rabbis, deceived by the pretenders, advocated it with enthusiasm, explicable only on the assumption that it surpassed their reason in strength.

The Frankists

The condition of the Jews in Germany cannot, like that of the Jews in Holland and other countries, be sketched in a few words. German territory was split up into minute divisions, each with its own ruler. If the Jew Lippold in Berlin, or the Jew Süss in Würtemberg succeeded in temporarily bettering the affairs of their coreligionists in their respective homes, that had no bearing upon the fortunes of the Jews elsewhere. In fact, they were banished from Berlin itself, returning thither after a century, as in so many cases, only in consequence of their misfortunes in another country, viz., in Austria. At the instance of his wife, Emperor Leopold I exiled them; in the year 1670 they had to leave Vienna. Three of the Viennese exiles, Benedict Veit, Abraham Lazarus, and Abraham Riess, went to Berlin to petition the Great Elector to throw open his dominions to the Jews. Frederick William, the enlightened monarch, granted their request, and in the next year seventy respected families, some of whose descendants still live there, moved to Berlin. Prussia had become a refuge of toleration and of religious liberty, the corner-stone upon which her greatness is built, which was soon to become the common heritage of all the nations. In 1671, then, the Jews again took up their abode in Berlin, and in 1714 the first public synagogue, the one in the *Heidereutergasse*, was solemnly dedicated in the presence of the king.

This brings us to the threshold of the modern epoch, the last period of our history. Let us take another backward glance at the condition of the Jews in the closing years of our fifth period. The picture is extremely sad, unillumined by a single ray of light. The traveller that would have chosen to make a tour of the Ghettos of Europe, from Constantinople by way of Warsaw to Frankfort and Leghorn, even to Rome, might have seen sights of unparalleled gloom. It is hardly credible, that the descendants of the old Maccabees, after having bid defiance to all persecutions and the efforts of centuries to crush the Jewish nation, should have sunk so low, become so degraded in carriage and language, so uncouth in habit and mind. At no point in the whole course of Jewish history do we meet with such degeneration as in the middle of the last century. *Degradation of the Jews*

So lamentably had they deteriorated, that Jews organized bandit companies, and rendered the roads unsafe. Was it possible, that a race dowered with intelligence, culture, and talent to produce a long line of celebrated poets and thinkers for the good of mankind, had so declined in language and life? The fact proves the possibility. But out of the lowest depth of degradation it was to be rescued by a movement, unequalled in force, which was to breathe new life into Judaism, and remind its adherents of the old mission repeated again and again in the Bible under manifold figures of speech, that Israel is called to be the witness of divine truth before all nations, and is to live as befits such a witness unto the end of all days, until the fate of the peoples of the earth shall have worked itself out.

If, then, Jewish history be studied closely and

with prophetic insight, we shall discover in it that which will renew and confirm our stubborn loyalty and justify the steadfastness of our faith in the realization of the ideals of Judaism. Our loyalty is rooted in the conviction that the ideals that transfigure our life have not yet been accepted by mankind. Even in our day the two great religious currents of which we have repeatedly had occasion to speak in these papers are flowing through the world in hostile separateness. So long as they do not mingle their waters, Israel's task is not accomplished. How the two views of life clash, the calendar often gives us the opportunity of observing in a curious way. Have my readers noticed in passing a Jewish house on many a winter evening the gleam of two sorts of lights? On the one side burn the Chanukkah candles, on the other, the lights of the Christmas tree—the ones the symbols of loyalty, the others, when shining forth from a Jewish house, the signs of thoughtlessness and faithlessness. Let us hold fast to the Chanukkah lights. They stand for unshaken faith in the ideals of Judaism, upon whose realization we hope and wait.

VI

In the thirty-seventh chapter of the book bearing the name of the prophet Ezekiel, we read of a wonderful vision, which is told somewhat in these words: "The hand of the Lord was upon me, and carried me out in the spirit of the Lord, and set me down in the midst of the valley which was full of bones. . . . And he said unto me, Son of man, can these bones live? And I answered, O Lord God, thou knowest. Again he said unto me, Prophesy upon these bones" . . . that they may live. And the spirit of God passed over them, and they became alive. The bones came together, bone to his bone; the sinews and the flesh came upon them, and the skin covered them above, and "they stood upon their feet an exceeding great army. Then he said unto me, Son of man, these bones are the whole house of Israel."

This prophetic vision recurs to our minds, when we study the sixth great period of Jewish history. And not this prophecy alone; many others, proclaimed over three thousand years ago, seem to have reached fulfilment. We are tempted to exclaim like Mother Zion of old: "Who hath begotten me these, seeing I have lost my children, and am desolate, a captive, and removing to and fro? and who hath brought up these? Behold, I was left alone; these, where had they been?" And Jeremiah spoke truth when

The Jewish Renaissance

he uttered the tender words: "Thus saith the Lord: I remember thee the kindness of thy youth, the love of thine espousals, when thou wentest after me in the wilderness, in a land that was not sown."

Yea, these promises received their brilliant fulfilment in Israel, who for thousands of years had wandered through deserts and wildernesses, always obeying the call of his God, always led by a holy inspiration, as it was called, but in reality pursuing a noble aim. A modern poet has described Israel's aim in beautiful words. Having passed Israel's history in review, he said: "A history like this cannot be an invention; it cannot be a lie. It is the greatest poem of all times, whose composition will probably continue until the last phase has been reached in the destiny of all the nations of earth."

How did the change come to pass? In the fifth paper, we left the Israelitish race in about the middle of the last century, the period of its lowest degradation. At no point in his changeful history had Israel sunk so low in respect of intellectuality, spirituality, religion, and morality as in the middle of the eighteenth century. Ignorant of the vernacular, excluded from public life, dependent upon the instruction of uncouth Polish teachers, without schools, without a suspicion of the glorious future destined for Israel, or of the glorious past he had lived through, slaves in aspect and in spirit—thus lived the Jews, and none could have imagined that so brilliant a Renaissance awaited them—a development so beautiful that it clamors for expression by the brush of a Michael Angelo or a Raphael.

Barely fifty years elapse, and the Jews in Berlin are leaders in social life and in literature; in France the public authorities declare the Jews citizens equal before the law to the other citizens; and in America we hear the Declaration of Independence, the proclamation of the equality of all men before the tribunal of God. What a change, what a miracle! No man, however great, could have brought about so complete a revolution single-handed. We see the footsteps of a higher Power, the one whose traces we have noticed again and again in the history of Israel, most plainly when Israel's distress was most dire.

The spirit of the Renaissance appears visibly incorporated in a boy of fourteen on a certain day of the last century. In 1743, a poor, trembling, misshapen lad knocked at the Rosenthal gate in Berlin, the only one by which Jews were permitted to enter the capital of Frederick the Great. To the clerk's question about his business in the city, he replied shyly: "Study." The boy was Moses Mendelssohn. Twenty years later, he submitted in competition for a prize offered by the Academy of Sciences an essay "On Evidence in Metaphysics," which aroused the admiration of the judges. At about the same time the boy who had been compelled to pay a poll-tax on entering Berlin because he was a Jew, took occasion to admonish the Ger-

Moses Mendelssohn

man nation to cherish its peculiar spiritual treasures more assiduously and not to deck itself with French tinsel. After another period of about twenty years, on his death, he was mourned by the world of letters and culture, and the greatest philosopher said: "There was but one Mendelssohn!" And no voice was heard to dissent from the praise given him by one of the greatest poets: "A sage like Socrates, faithful to the customs of the fathers, teaching immortality, immortal like him."

If it were possible to attribute the Renaissance to mortal agencies, we should have to lodge them in Moses Mendelssohn. He was no reformer, nor did he desire to become one. In his daily practice as in his views he held fast rigorously to the traditions of Judaism. He was, what is far more, the Germanizer of the German Jews. If one cared to compare him with Martin Luther, the comparison would, in a measure, be justified, since he did for German Jews what Luther had done for Germans in general: he gave them the Bible, and with the German Bible he gave them the German language, the German spirit, German life. Long before the Jews possessed political rights, they enjoyed equality in art, in letters, and in society. For this the Jews are indebted to Mendelssohn, and they should never grow oblivious of his deserts. Political offices, it must be admitted, were unattainable by them; even Frederick's "General Privilege" imposed numerous restrictions upon them. When Mendelssohn came to Berlin, the Jewish community frowned upon the reading of German books. A boy of fifteen, who had gone to fetch a German grammar for him, and was about to bring it to him, was caught in *Spandauerstrasse* by the overseer employed by the Berlin Jewish community to keep watch over the immigrant Jews. He took the book from the boy, roundly abused him, and procured his expulsion from Berlin. The little culprit was the grandfather of the late Gerson von Bleichrœder, the banker. Mendelssohn took him under his protection, and settled him in Halberstadt, where he continued his education at the German school, and later founded his famous banking establishment.

That is a little *genre* picture of the intellectual status of the Jews in Germany. Less than thirty years later it had ceased to be true to life. When Mendelssohn died, Henrietta Herz had already opened her *salon*, the meeting-place of all who had attained, or who gave promise of attaining, fame in German literature : the old rationalists, the leaders of the romanticism then in vogue, and the heads of the Young German movement, which obtained recognition a quarter of a century or more later. Before Moses Mendelssohn such a thing as sociability had been unknown in Berlin ; there were no social gatherings. A single *café* existed, at which the notabilities of the city met, and the castellan of the royal palace arranged *conversazioni* once or twice a week. That completes the description of Berlin society doings. Mendelssohn, only a poor book-keeper in the employ of the silk merchant

Isaac Bernhard, was the first to throw open his house hospitably. Poets, scholars, writers, poetesses, princesses, all persons of note in the world of letters who came to Berlin, frequented his drawing-room. Joachim H. Campe, the well-known author of " Robinson," has left us an attractive description of his afternoon at Mendelssohn's house, where a large company had gathered. It was in winter, when twilight sets in early. Mendelssohn disappeared, and when he returned, his wife became invisible. Suddenly the doors opened, and Frau Fromet Mendelssohn could be seen kindling the Sabbath lights and pronouncing the blessing over them. A feeling of holy awe, he continued, seized us, emanating from the spirit of the great philosopher, who had scaled the heights and explored the depths of thought, yet bowed humbly before his God. Moses Mendelssohn is not to be held responsible for the course of development taken by Judaism in Germany; he would have planned and recommended otherwise. Yet German Judaism owes him eternal gratitude. Like the first Moses, he liberated his people from Egyptian serfdom, and led them to spiritual heights. His contemporaries were not wrong in placing his name in proverbial connection with those of the two great Moses of earlier centuries.

The story goes, that one evening in the later years of his life Mendelssohn, who, as is well known, lived in the house 68 *Spandauerstrasse*, was found, anxiety depicted on his countenance, sitting under the tree at that time still shading the house. When asked by his friend, "What is the matter, Mr. Mendelssohn? Are you in trouble?" he answered, "I am thinking of the future of my children." Possibly, a breath of the spirit that later worked such disastrous effect upon Judaism was even then passing over Berlin. We meet with a phenomenon oft-repeated in history. The mind freed from the fetters of the prison house rushes blindly beyond the mark in its eagerness to reach the new and the good. The disciples, the children, and the friends of Mendelssohn did not pursue the path cleared by him; they deviated far from it. Intoxicated by the first draught from the cup of liberty proffered by the intellectual life of the period, they cast off the cloak that for thousands of years had afforded protection and warmth to the poor wanderers.

Berlin society was swayed in particular by the women among the Jews. We must draw a sharp distinction here between what the Jews gave the German people and the due they failed to pay their own race. Before we pass judgment upon the celebrated men and women of that day, we must be sure that we are bearing in mind the characteristics of the time in which their powers matured. On the one side, Judaism in its most hideous guise; ossified orthodoxy refusing entrance to the spirit of the times; repulsively ugly in form; disgusting, because its deeply religious essence was not recognized. On the other side, the exuberance of German intellectual life, the time of Frederick the Great, Immanuel Kant,

The Berlin Jewesses

Wolfgang Goethe, Friedrich von Schiller. At the parting of the ways the cultured Jews and Jewesses of Berlin stand, trying to choose between old, ugly Judaism, of whose beauty they had no conception, and German literature and life, which they absorbed naturally and joyously. Can we condemn them for the choice they made? At the utmost we may pity them for not having been granted insight into the profundity of Judaism. With a high degree of propriety, the Berlin Jews of the period were called "the Jews of Frederick the Great," and the best known literary critics have acknowledged, that much of what Berlin did for the furtherance of German intellectual and social life is due to the influence of its Jews.

Henrietta Herz, Dorothea Mendelssohn, the apostate daughter of a pious father, and Rachel Levin, supplied the new intellectual life with the germs of growth. When Rachel Levin became an enthusiastic Goethe admirer, fairly worshipping him as her god, she turned her back on Judaism. In a letter to Veit, she bewails her unhappiness: to have acquired so much culture, to have been endowed by God with so prophetic an insight into the future, and yet to have been sent into the world a Jewess! On her deathbed she spoke memorable words to her husband, Varnhagen von Ense, so weighty that he himself wrote them down in the sorrowful hour, when he was about to lose his adored wife forever. She said: "With sublime rapture I remember my origin and this whole chain of phenomena. What so long seemed only a sore disgrace, a bitter enemy, and a misfortune, my Jewish birth, under no consideration would I have it otherwise now."

We must retrace our steps somewhat. In the sixth period of Jewish history, leadership was assumed by the Judaism of Germany, but it would be erroneous to suppose, that the efforts to liberate the Jews from the bonds of servitude proceeded likewise from Germany. England was the original home of the emancipation movement. English freethinkers, especially John Toland, as early as the end of the seventeenth century declared the equal rights of all men on earth, since they all are created in the image of God. *The Emancipation of the Jews*

England recalled the Jews, and was the first country to grant them full liberty of worship. In 1776, America followed with the Declaration of Independence, and later came France with her Declaration of the Rights of Man, the equality of all men before the law, which afterwards suffered modification in this or that particular, especially in Alsace, but was never revoked for France as a whole. In fact, when Napoleon was enjoying the triumph of his victories, he thought that he was adding the greenest leaf to his crown of laurels by giving attentive care to the Jewish people. He assembled the Notables of the Jewish world in a Synhedrion, which was to renew the glory of the olden time, the heyday of Jewish national life. In 1807 the Synhedrion was opened with elaborate military festivities and all the pomp of the Napoleonic *régime*.

It was asked to consider twelve questions on the Jewish law of marriage and divorce and on the points of the Jewish civil code bearing particularly upon the relations between Jews and Christians, naturally of greatest interest to outsiders. The answers and the resolutions of the Synhedrion are matters of history. They are informed by the spirit of Judaism, unchanged since the earliest days: Judaism knows no hatred towards other nations; Judaism is free from envy of other religions; Judaism teaches love of man, faith in one God, and hope in the fraternization of all men. Such ideas and views necessarily produced a profound reaction in favor of the Jews in their relations to the various governments. The enlightened Austrian monarch, Joseph II, was the first to take these views into account in politics. Never before him had it been said, that Jews should be given the love and respect due to fellow men. Prussia was the last to take cognizance of the changed conditions. The Stein-Hardenberg edict, the seal and crown of the legislation by virtue of which Prussia became great, mighty, and influential in the council of the nations, gave expression to the propriety of emancipating the Jews. The hopes the Jews set in the edict were doomed to be blighted along with those of the whole German nation, and only in 1850 the equal rights of all religions were recognized in the constitution of Frederick William IV. The year 1871 finally removed the last obstacles theoretically in the way of the complete emancipation of the Jews.

Apparently the political history of the Jews has reached its close. In many states, to be sure, remnants may be met with of the old conditions, and not everywhere are Jews permitted to take a place in public life unchallenged. But we trust in the power of time, and this confidence is not a little strengthened, when we remember the enormous revolution that has taken place in the century and a half since the lad Mendelssohn in fear and trembling begged admittance to Berlin.

German Judaism, as I said above, assumed leadership in this last period of Jewish history, and the intellectual life of the Jews was as heavily freighted with important changes as their political fortunes. Abject degeneration was succeeded by a great upward development, whose impetus is to be sought in the free union between the Jewish and the German genius. The very Jews and Jewesses who became faithless to their religion at the beginning of this century—a large part of the Berlin Jewish community embraced Christianity—unconsciously to themselves and their more loyal brethren promoted the strivings of the Jewish spirit. Mendelssohn himself had entered into relations that exercised a favorable influence upon the future development of Judaism. It is well known, that he often visited the house No. 20 on the *Nikolaikirch-* Lessing and Mendelssohn *hof*, now 8 *Molkenmarkt*, to play chess, and that the chess-playing became the basis of a close, ardent, and enduring friendship, forever linking together two exalted minds, Mendelsson and Gotthold Ephraim Lessing. When Lessing wrote his "Nathan," he was obviously inspired by Moses Mendelssohn's character. In him he saw the ideal Jew, the incarnation of the spiritual ideal cherished by the great Jewish thinkers of all the centuries. The Jews thenceforth had a great task to accomplish. As Mendelssohn had united Jewish and Hellenic life, so it was for them to display before the eyes of a wondering world the Jewish spirit in all the vigor and ideality of its renewal.

Again the revival of Jewish intellectual life received its impetus at Berlin. The Jewish spirit had not yet spoken its last word; the time had not yet come for it to merge itself in the spirit of the other nations. The greater part of its mission was still unfulfilled. Realizing this truth, three Berlin Jews met in 1819 to found the Society for the Culture and the Science of the Jews: Edward Gans, Moses Moser, and Leopold Zunz. The society suffered wreck. Violating old custom and tradition, the captain was the first to leave the ship: in 1825 Gans, the president of the society, accepted baptism in order to become professor at Berlin. Zunz was the one who recognized what was to be rescued from out of the general chaos as the only possession calculated to secure the future position of Judaism. In a letter of his addressed to Immanuel Wohlwill, a member of the dead society, this memorable passage occurs: "The only thing that emerges from this chaos is the science of Judaism. It lives, though not a finger be raised in its behalf." Here for the first time the phrase, "the science of Judaism,"

The Science of Judaism

was uttered, and as it fell upon the ears of the world, the figure of Jewish science was seen to rise above the waters of the deluge, and the truth was borne in upon all beholders, that this same science had been the salvation of Judaism in the gloomy past, and that in the new era it would equip Judaism for the conflict with nations mightier and individuals stronger than its enemies of old. The science of Judaism issued from Germany. Distinguished scholars in all lands, in Poland, Italy, and France, flocked to its standard. Exacting respect, commanding reverence, equal to the sciences and the literatures of other nations, it challenges the criticism of all beholders, even of the renegades who had thought that Judaism had run its course, and who had said: "Come now, cast off your cloak. The breath of the new time is passing over us, and the nations are embracing us. Perish Judaism!"

The revival of Jewish science perforce carried with it a revival in the religious life. In the practice of the religion, however, unanimity did not prevail. **Reform and Orthodoxy** On the one side, it was maintained, that Judaism can preserve itself only by casting off a large portion of its old ceremonies, and particularly by rearranging the public divine service in a dignified and attractive way. The chief defender of this view was Abraham Geiger—in reverence his name be pronounced—a man of intense enthusiasm and deep devotion to the sacred cause. He formulated a program for Judaism from the point of view of the demands of the new era. The older men did not hang back;

they no longer were of the opinion, that Judaism was incompatible with the progress of the times. On the other side were men no less equipped with the culture of the century, yet filled with devoted love for the old traditions and customs. Their leader was Samson Raphael Hirsch, and his name, too, should be mentioned with respect. Both parties were filled with inspired enthusiasm for Judaism, and the honest motive of the one and of the other was to secure its perpetuity for themselves and those to come after them. The conflict of views and parties has never ceased—evidence that the Jewish mind neither wearies nor flags.

With the contest between the two religious parties we have reached the threshold of the present. It was erroneous to believe thirty or forty years ago, that the political history of the Jews had ended with the assimilation ardently promoted by them. The last twenty years everywhere on the globe have brought us grave disappointment; no less have they taught us a grave lesson. We know now, that our history has by no means come to an end; that the nations may not demand from us a complete surrender of Judaism as the price of complete citizenship; that in the future as in the past Judaism must pursue its own peculiar way. The storms now raging will pass, as others of their kind have passed. We who see everything, as Spinoza's phrase runs, *sub specie æternitatis,* from the point of view of eternity; we who stand on a watch-tower higher than the battlements of a modern party; we may indulge

[margin: Anti-Semitism.]

the confidence, that these storms, too, will blow over. We have weathered storms of worse kinds, and we have withstood enemies more powerful than the modern anti-Semites. We shall survive them as well. "Such a history," says Herder, "cannot be a lying invention; it is an unsolved riddle in the history of mankind."

We have arrived at our destination. It remains but to ask ourselves: What does the history of the Jews teach us? We have pursued the history through its six great periods, step by step, from the ancient beginnings, and we have emerged into the sunlight of the present. What has it all meant to us? For, surely, history is not to be studied for its own sake. Who considers history as nothing more than a list of numbers and dates, battles and revolutions, victories and names of kings, does not understand the real meaning of history. Profound lessons are to be drawn from history, for the world is ruled according to eternal laws, and the law operating in Jewish history is the belief in unalterable justice, unaffected by all the changes of the times, and from first to last dominant in the destiny of Israel.

Lesson of Jewish History

In the first book of the Bible we read a curious narrative. When the patriarch Jacob, after many years of exile from his home, was pursuing with yearning soul the road that led back to it, night overtook him, and a man assailed him and tried to kill him. Jacob wrestled with him through the night until the breaking of day. The combat exhausted him, but he did not yield. When morning dawned, the adversary said: "Let me go, for the day breaketh." Jacob replied: "I will not let thee go except thou bless me." And he blessed him, and called him Israel, champion of God. The sun had risen upon Jacob, and he thanked God, whose arm he had recognized.

In this simple account, we read, as it were, the whole history of the Jewish nation from its first origin in the Holy Land to its exile from its beloved home and its yearning to return thither. The long, dark night came, and with it the adversary, bringing Israel hatred, enmity, and contumely. While the darkness lasted, Israel wrestled with him, and though the struggle often drained his strength, he was not conquered, for faith ever sustained his courage. And when the morning dawned, the adversary said: "Let me go, for the day breaketh." But Israel said: "I will not let thee go except thou bless me. It is not enough that thou hast left off from thy hostility towards me. I will not let thee go until thou givest me thy love and ownest me thine equal." Judaism would not have the right to demand love, if it had not been ever ready to treat the nations of the earth with love.

When we scan the marvellous history of Judaism, we are struck by a remarkable phenomenon, a tragic-comical phenomenon, I am tempted to call it. On one side, offering defiance to a whole world ranged on the other side, stands a small, insignificant band of men, a spiritual power, never weary, never disheartened, always maintaining its individuality. Maintaining its individuality for what? The purpose is expressed in the history of the tiny band. In the narrative from Genesis, Jacob is called champion of God, and that Israel must continue to be now and ever. Israel's mission is not yet fulfilled. Were it fulfilled, the world were a different place. Certain as it is, that in the last great struggle between the races of men Judaism will stand its ground, provided we do not lose from our consciousness the belief in our mission, to teach the world the knowledge of the one God (for even to-day the majority of mankind are heathen); so certain is it, that the time will come, when all the heathen, when every knee will bend before God, and all men will recognize that He is one unto the end of days. So long as religions exist, Judaism will exist. When all religions will have united, the religion of the prophets will prevail—the religion consisting of the acknowledgment of *one* God in heaven above, the Ruler of the world, and of *one* realm on the earth below, the realm of fraternal love, humanity, liberty, and justice.